Teaching Martial Arts

Other martial arts books available from A & C Black

Applied Tai Chi Chuan by Nigel Sutton
Elite Karate Techniques by David Mitchell
Injury-free Karate by Paul Perry
Jiu Jitsu by Professor Robert Clark
Judo Games by Geof Gleeson
Judo Inside Out by Geof Gleeson
The Martial Arts Coaching Manual by David Mitchell
Martial Arts Injuries by Dr James Canney
Mobility Training for the Martial Arts by Tony Gummerson
Okinawan Karate by Mark Bishop
The Police Self-Defence Handbook by Brian Eustace
Self Defence for All by Fay Goodman
Skilful Karate by Greg McLatchie
Strength Training for the Martial Arts by Tony Gummerson
**Training Theory for Martial Arts* by Tony Gummerson
Winning Karate Competition by David Mitchell
**Yang Tai Chi Chuan* by John Hine

*In preparation

Teaching Martial Arts

Tony Gummerson

A & C Black · London

First published 1992 by
A & C Black (Publishers) Ltd
35 Bedford Row, London WC1R 4JH

ISBN 0 7136 3399 9

A CIP catalogue record for this book is available from the British Library.

Acknowledgements
Line drawings by Taurus Graphics.

Typeset in Monophoto Joanna by
August Filmsetting, Haydock, St Helens.

Printed and bound in Great Britain by
BPCC Hazells Ltd
Member of BPCC Ltd

Contents

Acknowledgements

To produce a coaching manual such as this requires the help and expertise of a great many people. There are particular individuals who deserve a special word of thanks.

Wilf Paish, former British Athletic Federation National Coach, mentor and adviser to Olympic champions and numerous international athletes, directed my own international sporting activities and planted the seed of desire to become an equally effective coach.

Carl Johnson, British Athletic Federation National Coach, who has perhaps more than anyone created a professional approach to coaching both in the U.K. and other countries, gave me the opportunity and support to develop my understanding of the coaching process.

Many martial-arts governing bodies have given me the opportunity to learn from them.

Finally, can I thank all of the sportsmen and women who have been gracious enough to place their sporting destiny in my hands over the past 20 years. They have provided me with the opportunity to put theory into practice.

Author's note

The current trend in sport and recreation is to use the word 'coach' when referring to the person who imparts his knowledge and expertise to those who wish to learn and benefit from them. Within the martial arts the term 'coach' is used along with 'instructor', 'teacher' and 'trainer', and a whole range of terms of respect and authority in the language of the country of origin of a particular style, 'sensei' or 'seefoo' for example. Throughout the book the term 'coach' is used predominantly. Where 'instructor', 'teacher' and 'trainer' are used, the same meaning as 'coach' is intended unless otherwise specified.

Also, throughout the book coaches and students are referred to individually as 'he'. This should of course be taken to mean 'he or she' where appropriate.

'The main task in coaching is to convince and inspire. The truly great coach lives his message, looks the part; his whole demeanour proclaims his belief in what he says. He is devoted to his art; for without devotion of some kind nothing great was ever achieved.'

Geoff Dyson

I

The development of coaching

The history of the more popular martial arts that are practised today throughout the world goes back many centuries, their origins firmly based in the Orient. The interest that many students have in such activities is not only directed towards the acquisition and development of effective fighting techniques, but also towards the mythology, tradition and historical development of their particular style. Most students are similarly curious about the art, sculpture, music, culture and history of its country of origin. Martial-arts students are especially interested in the evolution of their particular style into its present form. Among the many leisure activities and sports that are played and practised today, this sense of all-embracing interest and curiosity exhibited by most martial artists in their chosen activity is very rare.

Traditionally the martial arts have a particular practice – that sets them apart from other sports and activities – that evolved from their cultural and historical development. There was an established practice in the teaching of techniques by the instructor, who was usually referred to as 'the master' by the student. Any instruction was based on the assumption that the master was himself a highly successful and skilful martial artist. The competence that the master had in instructing others was dependent on his own personal expertise in a variety of combat situations and training experiences. Traditionally the various fighting techniques and associated skills were passed on in this fashion. There was much to commend this practice in that a great deal of knowledge and techniques were passed on from master to student. However, it did not always follow that it was done in the most effective manner.

Very often the student would be a favoured individual or relative of the master. Anyone who wanted to be taught had to show that he was worthy spiritually, mentally and physically of the rigours of training. Long periods, perhaps years, of menial work, subservience to the master and adherence to spiritual, cultural and social discipline frequently preceded the training process. Often during the teaching process the master would not fully explain a technique. The student had to elevate his mind to develop a 'harmony' with the thoughts of the master to achieve what was required. The very ability to attune to the master's values and motives was seen to be the most important element of the learning process. Most of the martial arts were taught on the basis of this 'non-teaching' method. This strategy required an unwillingness to analyse what was to be taught or the method by which it was to be presented to the student. This non-teaching practice allowed the student to be free to understand without being constrained, but it also absolved the master of all blame if things went wrong: 'the student did not understand'!

In recent years the more enlightened martial artists have realised that the technical competence and competitive success that an individual has is no measure of his ability to teach any skills and knowledge that he possesses to others. There is a large amount of information now available, especially in the martial arts, that seems to indicate the élite performers do not necessarily make the most effective teachers. A recent survey of martial-arts instructors who had competed at the highest level internationally showed that they were not equally successful in being able to attract and keep students in their clubs. To grade to the highest levels in any style requires a great deal of natural ability, motivation, commitment, dedication and hard work. Possessing this facility for learning and refining techniques and skills does not always give élite performers an understanding of those lesser mortals whose natural abilities, tenacity and dedication are not so highly developed. Furthermore, they often find difficulty in understanding the problems experienced by these less gifted and committed students in training, grading and competition. The many years of training in and association with any martial art must not be taken as a guide to the ability or competence of any individual to teach others.

Out of the custom of the élite martial artist teaching his students has emerged a great deal of myth and mystery. There has always been secrecy surrounding the techniques and training methods of most martial arts. Each master would have his own repertoire of techniques that he felt were particularly important. Obviously, skills that were effective in the combat, competition or training environment were retained, while those that were not were discarded. It was felt that these skills should not be revealed to those outside that particular style. It is only in recent years that observation, photography or filming of the various fighting styles has been allowed. Historically, if the master of a style wanted to test the effectiveness of his particular techniques, he would issue a challenge to another master. Often the loser, feeling disgraced (especially if he had issued the challenge), would commit suicide. The implications of losing such a challenge tended to reinforce the secrecy surrounding training and techniques. Obviously it would not have been wise for a master to allow an opponent to have an in-depth understanding of his techniques, or any advantage would be lost, possibly along with his life!

Traditionally, unswerving loyalty to both the master and the style was required from all students. The problem, however, was that there was little, if any, cooperation or exchange of knowledge between the different martial arts and instructors in particular, and other sports and activities in general. This very sterile state of affairs did not allow for the interchange of new techniques, training practices and teaching styles, which would have been advantageous for the overall development of the activity.

There are tremendous differences between the way the more popular styles are practised now compared with the past. Our perception of training is based on the refinement of what were initially techniques for combat to kill and maim to today's more stylised forms, which are no doubt equally effective. Because of this cloak of secrecy surrounding the teaching of the various styles, there has been little in the way of comprehensive instructional manuals or illustrative material. There is much in the way of social histories and anecdotal accounts and drawings, but more specific insights into training, techniques and any other special practices are rare.

Despite their various shortcomings and the apparent lack of long-term planning and objectivity, the development of martial arts has been quite impressive. Since the 1960s there has been a rethink of the training methods that sportsmen and women use to achieve excellence. Theories of training that have been developed predominantly in eastern European countries have probably been the most significant influence. The past 20 years in particular have also seen a major change in our life-styles. More leisure time and increased affluence have brought about a large rise in the number of participants in sport in general and the martial arts in particular. More recently an awareness of the importance of exercise for improving health and preventing illness and debilitating disease has helped to swell the numbers of students. With the desire to achieve ever-higher levels of performance and to make the best possible use of training time, participants in sport and leisure activities have been quick to see the advantages of the application of developments in medicine, science and technology. In their search for ever-improving levels of performance, teachers and students of the martial arts now regularly seek the help of the various sports scientists.

By their very nature, the martial arts require a high degree of technical proficiency and skill. The present level of excellence in the martial arts is mainly due to the traditional methods of instruction and training. However, a much more efficient, effective and ultimately successful approach could be achieved more generally if the appropriate disciplines of the sports sciences were studied and, where relevant, incorporated. The present success of the martial arts, based on their traditional practices, has been achieved despite rather than because of these practices, but their continued development will depend on the ability of the various fighting styles to take on board new ideas and methods. An open-minded situation will create a climate that will not only allow the martial arts to flourish but will also give each and every student the opportunity to achieve his full potential.

However, the martial arts must not be complacent in their attitude to their coaching activities. Success in terms of international honours and total numbers of students in regular training comes at a price. There is tremendous 'wastage' in the number of students who 'drop out' of training, see Fig. 1. This situation cannot truly reflect activities that are

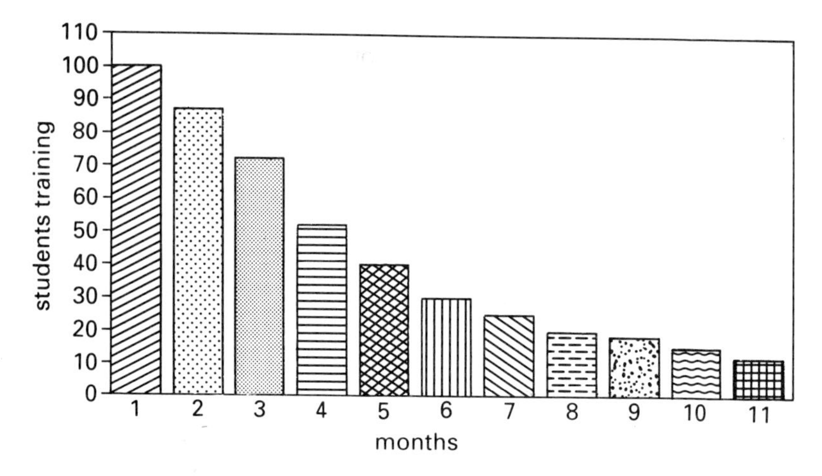

Fig. 1 The student 'drop-out' curve: out of every 100 students who take up a martial art, at the end of 12 months less than 15 are still training

attractive to individuals of different ages and abilities who seek different requirements from their association with a particular style. The founder of shotokan karate, Master Funakoshi Gichin, said 'The ultimate aim of the art of karate lies not in victory or defeat, but in the perfection of the character of its participants'.

Those sentiments are still relevant today, and are common to most, if not all, of the popular fighting styles. However, many individuals will never benefit from all that the martial arts have to offer. They stop training before they have appreciated and come to value what each style can give them. Perhaps a review of coaching methods by the various styles might help to prevent the present high loss of students.

2

What's in a name?

One of the many difficulties with the martial arts is terminology. Some martial arts give all instruction and names in the mother tongue of the country of origin, such as Japanese, Chinese, Korean or Thai. If that were not confusing enough, many coaches of the martial arts adopt different titles such as 'sensei', 'seefoo' and 'professor'. However, to cloud the issue even more, if asked what their role is in a martial art they might describe themselves in English as an 'instructor', 'teacher', trainer' or 'coach'. Often these terms are used synonymously when in fact they do not mean the same thing; they are very different. The confusion is compounded by one reference work that gives the following definitions:

- instructor; one who teaches
- teacher; one who instructs
- trainer; one who prepares animals to perform tricks!
- coach; one who gives instruction.

It can be quite clearly understood why there is so much confusion over which title a martial-arts 'communicator of skills and knowledge' might choose!

Often the descriptive term chosen is very revealing about the style of communication in general and the values of the martial art in particular.

The instructor

Some martial arts attract large classes, often with in excess of 30 students. With most facilities there is an organisational problem of accommodating all of the group and ensuring that they train in safety. In this situation any form of training has to ensure that all students execute the same technique or sequence at the same time. For example, all students move forwards or in any direction at the same time. By ensuring that students move *en bloc*, a safe learning environment is created. With such training the movements are normally drills or the repetition of techniques. All activity is controlled by commands or orders. There is no potential for any student to deviate from the class practice. Any such variance could lead to injury.

With such large numbers, there is no opportunity for individual student–instructor contact. It is a very impersonal form of communication. It may well be that the instructor who finds personal relationships difficult prefers to work in this manner. Similarly, some students prefer to seek anonymity in a large, impersonal group, as no one singles them out or places them in an 'exposed' and possibly embarrassing situation.

The teacher

The problem with instruction is that there is no interaction between student and instructor. This is not the case with teaching. For example, a student might need to ask questions about a technique, or the teacher might need to give feedback as to the quality of training. This is difficult, if not impossible, with large numbers. There is much more of a working relationship, which obviously requires the teacher to relate effectively with individuals. Furthermore, it might take on another dimension with the teacher acting as a confidant with respect to the personal problems of a student that might, or might not, have an effect on learning and refinement of techniques. The teacher finds himself being very sensitive to the individual needs and problems of the students. It is important to bear in mind that it is people who are taught personal and technical skills. They are the most important aspect of any martial art. The techniques are the vehicle by which improvements are brought about.

Teachers are interested in the overall development of their students and must be prepared to take on board the responsibility of creating and cultivating relationships. Similarly, students must be prepared in this form of learning environment to relate to the teacher to gain the most from the lesson.

The trainer

With training, the aim of any activity is geared towards the development of excellence of performance as a result of improvements in both technique and fitness. The trainer becomes a motivator and disciplinarian to ensure that his students work to the best of their ability at all times. There is little in the way of interaction between the trainer and the pupil. The student is there to work and absorb as much of the trainer's experience and knowledge as possible. As the student has absolute confidence in the ability of his trainer, there is no need for discussion. This kind of learning environment does not lend itself to close relationships between trainer and pupil. It tends to depend upon the ability of the student to adhere to the strict discipline required to achieve excellence by being obedient to the trainer's wishes. However, a trainer working in this way can supervise the activities of a small group.

The coach

The coach's sole concern is the student's ability to achieve his potential, no matter at what level. The coach is equally interested that novice, mature, slow-learning and gifted pupils should achieve the highest standard of which they are able. This means that very small groups or individual attention is required. It also means that the coach, in order to get the best out of his students, has to have a very close relationship with them. This form of learning can be very satisfying but equally very demanding for student and coach alike.

In this style of learning the coach has to become an instructor, teacher and trainer as the situation demands. Similarly, the student has to be able to cope with the anonymity of 'instruction', the questioning of 'teaching', the discipline of 'training' and the undivided attention of the coach in a one-to-one situation.

However, the real world is not quite as clear-cut as described. This is because in every lesson each one of the styles of communication would be found, see Fig. 2. For example, at the start of the lesson and during the warm-up and class activities (in which the whole group work together), instruction is required. As the lesson develops with the class dividing into small groups, teaching is required. As feedback is given to individual

instruction	**teaching**	**training**	**coaching**
predetermined commands; activity is usually drills	opportunity to develop skills in a variety of situations	development of élite performance	development and attainment of a student's potential

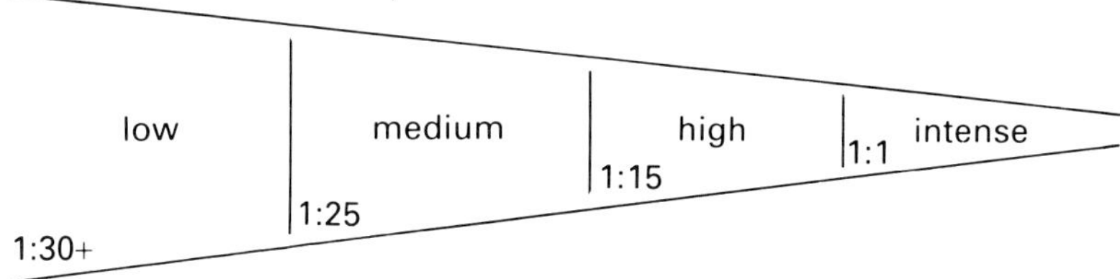

Fig. 2 Styles of communication: different styles of communication relate to the number of students

students, coaching is required. If there is a need for the development of technique or specific fitness, training is required.

The situation is further clarified, or muddied, by the advent of a much closer liaison with the rest of Europe. The British Institute of Sports Coaches has identified a 'coach' as: 'Anyone who coaches, teaches or gives instruction but not a full-time education professional or an administrative director of coaching'. It has defined 'coaching' as: 'The process of imparting techniques, skills, knowledge and attitude aimed at improving the performance of the individual using methods appropriate to their ability and aspirations'.

It does seem that the B.I.S.C. has attempted to resolve the confusion of the various terms. It sees 'coaching' as an all-embracing term that adopts all of the communication strategies that an expert might use in order to pass on to others his knowledge and expertise.

It is clear that the specific title that an 'instructor', 'teacher', 'trainer' or 'coach' may claim is an all-embracing one that in truth encompasses all of the various communication strategies and regimes that have been identified. Other titles such as 'professor', 'master', 'sensei', 'seefoo' or any other must be regarded as a variant of those identified, with a particular emphasis on respect and endearment.

Just to throw a further spanner into the works, recently I was informed that there is another title to consider – that of 'martial-arts consultant'! At a time when an individual's professional credentials are very important, why shouldn't an expert in a martial art offer his skills through a 'consultancy'? After studying and training for seven years or more, is he not worthy of the same kind of status as an accountant, surveyor or solicitor? Perhaps there is a lesson to be learned here. In other sports such as golf, tennis, squash and swimming a coach has both kudos and status, as well as professional recognition of his expertise. Though the training and preparation of martial-arts 'experts' may be longer and more intensive than any of the professional and sporting examples given, it is clear that in no way do such experts have the same status or respect from the general public.

Again, perhaps it is the fault of the martial arts, which have been prepared to let the more spectacular and – dare one say – more disreputable image be publicised. Whereas this situation may have added more to the myth of the martial arts, it has done very little to enhance their true nature or the level of expertise and excellence of those who have taken on board the onerous task of promoting their worth and coaching others.

3

Who wants to be a coach?

There can be little doubt that in today's western society there is an ever-increasing demand for 'value for money'. This philosophy does not deal only with the materialistic aspects of life such as food, clothes, cars, houses or services; it also includes sport and leisure. Within the category of 'sport and leisure' can be found all of the martial arts. This materialistic and mercenary attitude of the western civilisations may be at odds with that of the eastern cultures, where the more popular martial arts evolved, but it must be recognised.

Traditionally the martial arts as taught in the Orient are pervaded by religious and philosophical values that may be paramount. However, in western culture these values may be of secondary importance. If I buy a car I want value for money. I am not interested in the religious or philosophical values of the company, or of the workers who made it. As far as I am concerned it needs to meet all of the advertised economic and mechanical specifications that it offers. Similarly, if I attend an educational, professional or vocational course that will give me the knowledge and understanding to acquire a qualification, I expect to attain that qualification. So too with coaching: if I give my very valuable free time, and pay to study a particular martial art, I expect to learn and develop those skills.

It may be well and good to accept the eastern attitude that the student will develop as an individual through the training process, but unfortunately in the West this is not good enough; we need to see results. In the East there was often no grading system, the student studying for many years before being rewarded with a token of technical competence, which was not always a 'black belt'. In the West, however, perhaps to satisfy our flagging egos and constantly ensure value for money, we need reassurance that we are improving. To meet this need (to a large extent) the grading systems common to most, if not all, of the more important martial arts were developed. However, linked to this progression in technical competence has emerged a strange practice. It is assumed that once a student has achieved a particular level of *personal* competence, usually black belt or its equivalent, suddenly he is able to effectively pass his knowledge on to other students.

In today's society it is no longer acceptable that a student's personal level of performance automatically enables him to be an effective teacher.

Where is the professional training programme that enables the competent student to learn the vital communication techniques to allow him to pass on the knowledge that he possesses to others? In all truth it is only in the last few years that the problem has been addressed and an education programme has been available to coaches of the various martial arts. However, there are many thousands of coaches already established in the martial arts, with many more who want to take on that role, who may be unaware of the responsibilities and duties necessary for effective and efficient instruction.

You, the coach or aspiring coach, have to ask yourself some very important questions as to your motives and reasons for wanting to coach.

- Who asked you to become a coach?
- What makes you think that you can coach?
- Do you have the technical skills to be a coach?
- Do you have the personal skills to be a coach?
- Are you prepared to accept the responsibility of being a coach?

Unfortunately society and the public expect a certain standard of competence from 'experts' in sport in general and especially in the potentially dangerous environment of the martial arts. The general question that you must ask yourself is quite simple,

- Do you have the necessary technical and communicational skills to coach?

The level of technical proficiency that a coach has is a measure of his level of fighting skills, not of his ability to teach. In the following sections the necessary skills required to become an effective coach will be identified. If they are incorporated into a coaching programme, along with your own personality, technical competence and knowledge of your style of martial art, a most effective teaching and learning environment will be created. This will be to the benefit of you, the students and ultimately the martial art itself.

4

Coach education and the martial arts

Although participation in the martial arts in western society was established at the turn of the century, and some might argue long before that, the umbrella representative body in the UK, the Martial Arts Commission of Great Britain, only came into being as recently as 1977. Prior to the setting up of the Martial Arts Commission (M.A.C.) in Great Britain and of similar representative bodies in other countries, 'governing bodies', 'federations' and 'associations' of the different fighting styles functioned totally independently. Being autonomous, they were able to establish their own standards of technical competence through their grading systems and to accredit their own coaches.

However, there were two problems with this situation. Firstly, there was little, if any, comparability of technical competence with similar grades in different styles. And, secondly, there was little 'quality control' of the competence and effectiveness of coaches.

The Martial Arts Commission of Great Britain, as an example, was set up as a representative organisation in 1977 to act, among other things, as a self-regulatory body and to agree acceptable safety standards, levels of technical competence and coaching standards throughout the member bodies. One of the ways in which it began to introduce quality control was to affirm the technical ability of affiliated coaches.

In 1984 the M.A.C. proposed that they bring their organisation into line with the other sports governing bodies in the United Kingdom and throughout the world generally and that they implement a comprehensive Coach Education Programme. The then embryonic National Coaching Foundation (N.C.F.), which was set up in 1983, was closely involved in this process. The N.C.F. has undertaken a comparative study of coaching programmes throughout the world, particularly in Canada, the U.S.A. and the Eastern bloc countries. Officers of the N.C.F. travel all over the world, attending seminars and conferences, and setting out the need for and presenting comparable standards. They also take full advantage of the expertise of coach educators from these countries. Through its continued association with these and other national coaching bodies, the N.C.F. has established an international reputation and has created a coach education model which has been widely adopted.

Most of the major sports governing bodies have identified four levels

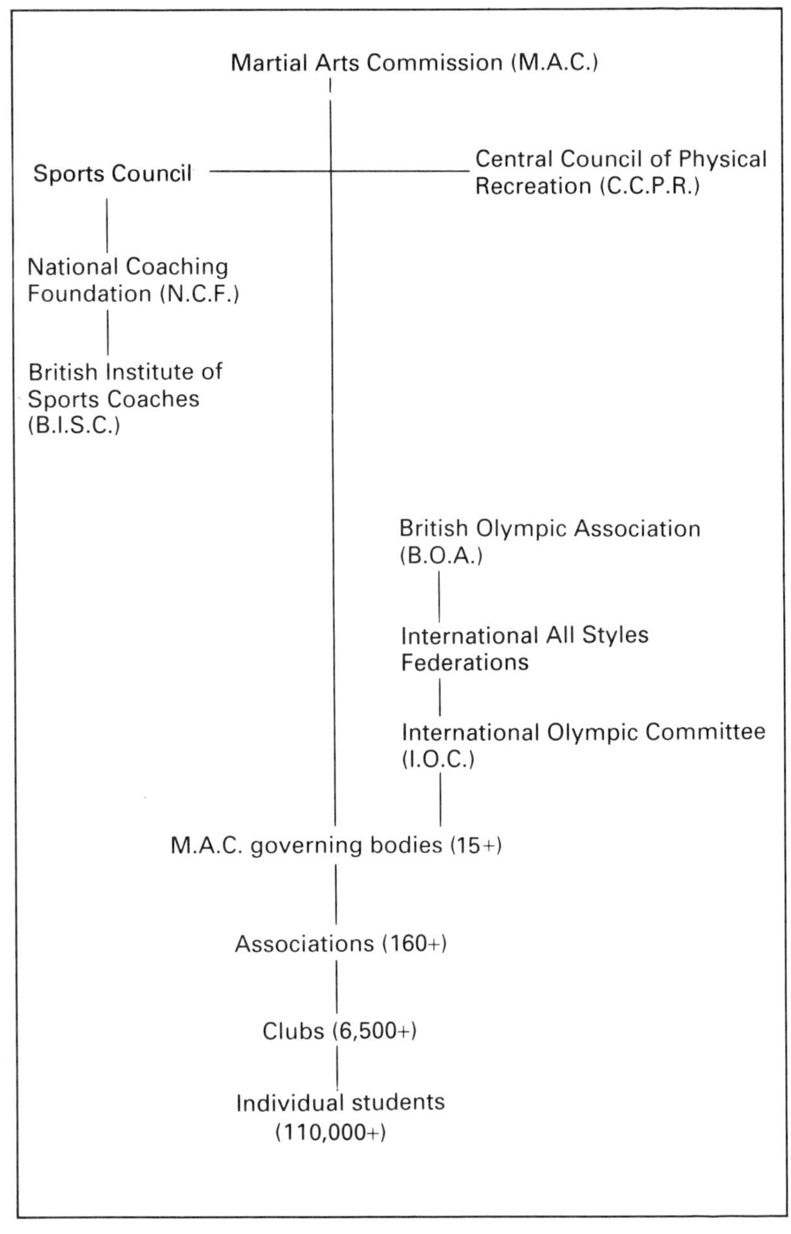

Fig. 3 The national and international structure of the M.A.C.: the M.A.C. is the representative body for martial arts and serves the needs of its constituent associations and governing bodies

of coaching expertise. Since the Sports Council in the U.K., through the National Coaching Foundation, were themselves suggesting a similar structure it seemed obvious to construct a comparable programme for the martial arts. When the nature of the various elements in each level was discussed by people from different sports, it was interesting to note that the same requirements for the education of coaches were identified independently by all of the governing bodies.

However, from the very start there was more than a little resistance from the martial arts to the coaching programme. This was not just because it seemed to threaten the autonomy and tradition of particular styles. To be perfectly honest, there was some justification for the concern. One of the biggest problems with the Coach Education Programmes of the 160 or so different sports governing bodies and associations recognised by the Sports Council lay in the simple fact that most of them had no requirement for a personal standard of performance, let alone excellence, on the part of the coach. I suspect that this situation may be common in many other countries as well. Putting it simply, it was quite possible to become a National Coach, or indeed a coach at one of the lower levels, without ever having participated in the activity at all either as a competitor or as a performer.

In activities such as athletics, swimming and gymnastics, coaching can be purely theoretical and as such the need for a comprehensive coach education programme has been both well-received and supported. However, in these programmes not all the information is sport-specific; as much as 50% of the time is devoted to the development of management, communication and coaching skills. It is not enough to have a body of knowledge to be a successful coach; the ability to pass on those skills to others in such a way that each and every sportsperson can achieve their potential, at whatever level, is essential.

The movement forwards by the various martial arts towards a coaching structure was helped by the fact that there already existed a form of training for potential coaches. Traditionally, a student worked his way through the grading system before becoming a coach. He might take up to seven years to achieve the black belt, or first dan, or whichever level was identified as indicating a competence to instruct others. Obviously those coaches who went through this process developed a high degree of excellence in their particular style and had personal experience of the highs and lows of training, grading and competition. However, to achieve an élite standard of personal performance usually requires a fair amount of natural ability, motivation and commitment. It does not follow that an élite martial artist also has the ability to pass those skills on to others at all levels. In fact, the opposite is usually true. To become an élite performer usually means the student has natural ability and there-

Students of the martial arts come in all ages and sizes, and have a multitude of reasons for taking up a particular style

fore learns skills easily and quickly. A great degree of self-motivation and commitment is also required and such performers generally find little difficulty in applying themselves to the rigours of training, grading and competition. Since very few students achieve such high levels of performance, too often a coach does not understand the needs of these 'lesser mortals' who are in fact in the majority. When one looks at specific groups such as junior, female, male, elderly, competitive, non-competitive, aggressive, shy, introverted, or combinations of these, many martial arts coaches in the past have been, to say the least, under-prepared.

The success of the various coaching elements of the martial arts has been based, certainly in coaching terms, on trial and error! The current group of excellent coaches are those who have been instructing for several years. In that time they have taught both good and bad lessons and have learned what does, and more importantly what does not, work when teaching different 'types' of martial arts students. It is with this group of coaches that a misunderstanding of the M.A.C. Coach Education Programme has developed. There has been a notion of 'I've been coaching martial arts for 20 years. What can they teach me?'

As has been identified, probably very little, if anything at all. In fact, if they were to be exposed to any 'new' ideas, it would be very surprising, since all that they should pick up from the courses is confirmation that what they have identified as safe, efficient and effective coaching is actually recognised as good practice.

The whole purpose of a Coach Education Programme is to short-circuit that potentially very dangerous learning process by identifying to embryonic coaches safe, effective and efficient coaching practices from the outset, without exposing them to the possible pitfalls and dangers of a trial and error process of 'experimental learning'. The strength of the current Coach Education Programme, together with a high level of personal skills and an indepth knowledge of the demands on a student, will elevate the overall quality of coaching to a standard higher than most, if not all other, governing bodies affiliated to the Sports Council and National Coaching Foundation!

It is interesting to note that there is to be a requirement for coaches outside the European Community to meet the same criteria of competence. Controversially, it will also include leading oriental exponents, the 'Grand Masters' of their particular style. It will no longer be enough to be venerated and held in high regard by students. To resolve this problem there is a growing interest in internationally accepted standards. This, of course, will include sports coaching and will enable a coach to work anywhere within the E.C. To ensure that there is a recognised standard of coaching, the Sports Council, The British Institute of Sports Coaches, the N.C.F. and the various government agencies have defined who will be recognised as an accredited coach. A definition which the N.C.F. has put forward for insurance purposes is an excellent attempt to identify the competence and status of coaches: *A COACH IS DEFINED AS ANY PERSON WHO HOLDS A CERTIFICATE OF COACHING ISSUED BY THE NATIONAL GOVERNING BODY OF HIS OR HER SPORT OR WHO HOLDS A RECOGNISED EDUCATIONAL QUALIFICATION AS A TEACHERE WITH A SPECIALISATION IN PHYSICAL EDUCATION.*

There is no doubt that this state of affairs will be closely monitored and enforced in the U.K. and in Europe generally. The legislation and the will already exist through 'The Health and Safety at Work Act'. Indeed, some local authorities have already appointed individuals to 'police' local coaches and to ensure that only those who are qualified under the new legislation are allowed to operate. It is further planned that unqualified coaches will be unable to obtain insurance cover for their clubs and associated activities. To give an extreme example of the implementation of such schemes, in January of 1990 the French police arrested all the unqualified Ski Instructors at several resorts! The implication for the various governing bodies inside and outside the M.A.C. and similar bodies throughout Europe and the rest of the world is obvious. The days of the disreputable organisation and instructor are rapidly coming to an end.

A coach education programme for the martial arts

The demands of coaching today far outstrip the historical picture of the master teaching his skills and knowledge over a period of many years to only one or two students. The economic constraints of running a financially viable club require large numbers of students to train together. There is of course the social and practical need of students being able to train in moderately large groups. Putting it simply, modern coaches work with more students for a considerably shorter period of time than before. This of course makes much greater demands upon their technical ability and communication and organisational skills.

Since the presentation of the initial concept in 1984 and the introduction of the Martial Arts Commission's Coach Education Programme in 1986, many courses have been organised throughout Great Britain, aimed at covering various levels of coaching ability. The content of the various courses leading to awards has been discussed at length to arrive at the present elements. There is really little opportunity for great variations in structure and content, as there has to be comparability with other sports-governing-body awards at the various levels. And, neither should there be! Good practice in coaching the martial arts has many of the same requirements as good coaching in other sports and leisure activities. The techniques may be different but the communicational, organisational and management skills required to create the best teaching and learning environment are much the same.

The main aim of any Coach Education Programme is to identify an efficient and effective system of coaching. Fundamental to any administrational or organisational skills are of course the individual governing bodies' grading structure and the internal means of student and coach development. Both of these factors may have a profound effect on the teaching situation.

Components of the programme

Without being too specific, the following guidelines identify some of the attributes of good practice in coaching that should be encompassed in coach education programmes.

Assessing the situation

- Being aware of the varied requirements and expectations of the students, which are affected by such variables as age, gender, ability and general health.
- Being aware of the differing physical and psychological demands of the various styles.
- Being aware of the differing physical and psychological demands on the student in the training, grading and competitive environment.
- Keeping up-to-date with current trends in techniques and in training, grading and competition.
- Keeping abreast of current policy within the governing body and the martial arts specifically, and sport and leisure in general.

Planning the programme

- Planning the long-term training to allow students of all abilities to achieve their potential.
- Making the fullest use of available technical and facility resources.
- Keeping accurate records on the development of students and being aware of specific dates and information that might influence the training programme.

Implementing the programme

- Organising and monitoring the long-term coaching programme for each student.
- Planning and teaching the individual lessons that make up the programme.
- Developing communication skills with students and all other individuals involved.
- Creating and developing personal and professional relationships with other individuals and organisations.
- Managing facilities and other coaches to facilitate the implementation of the coaching programme.

Analysing the programme

- Being able to constructively analyse each training, grading or competition session.
- Being able to constructively analyse the work of other coaches and organisations.
- Being able to constructively analyse the effectiveness of the overall coaching programme.

Specific martial-arts components

All of the above elements are not only requirements for effective coaching in all of the various styles of martial arts but, as previously identified, they are common to most sports and leisure activities. With specific reference to the martial arts, the units can be grouped in various ways.

The martial arts, generally and specifically

- Being aware of the present structure of the martial arts at a national level.
- Knowing the philosophy and traditions of the particular style.
- Assessing the place of martial arts in society.
- Being aware of the recruitment pattern of students.
- Resourcing effective teaching and learning.
- Considering the benefits of participation in the martial arts within the total education of the student.

Organisation and administration

- Devising and implementing a long-term training programme.
- Establishing and maintaining students' standards of dress, behaviour, attitude and commitment.
- Implementing safety regulations and accident procedures.
- Ensuring regular tuition.
- Devising a system to reward excellence and impose sanctions where appropriate.
- Arranging extra training where appropriate.
- Arranging for grading and competitions.
- Ordering equipment for students.
- Arranging and managing training camps and competition trips and tours.
- Communicating with governing bodies, the media and other agencies.
- Offering representation on committees and at meetings.

Staffing

- Influencing the development of an association.
- Going on in-house association or governing-body courses.
- Attending courses run by outside agencies.
- Being aware of developmental needs.
- Being aware of association needs.

The four levels

The Coach Education Programme of the Martial Arts Commission is both comprehensive and structured to include all of the necessary elements to produce efficient, effective and safe training, grading and competition. The programme falls into four levels of coaching competence, the requirements of which are outlined below.

A foundation course covering basic coaching skills

This is intended for the aspiring coach on the first rung of the coaching ladder, who assists the class teacher. The first level of coaching involves 'workplace' experience under the watchful eye of a senior coach, during which the embryonic coach develops the following skills:

- work closely with and under the supervision of the class coach
- demonstrate and explain basic techniques
- identify errors and suggest methods of correction
- give feedback to the students
- reinforce good performance with praise
- adapt a teaching style to suit different situations
- develop an effective working relationship with students
- ensure maximum participation and enjoyment
- prepare students for training
- cool down students after training.

A basic coaching award

After gaining both experience and confidence, the aspiring coach might want to develop the skills required to teach a class without the constant supervision of another coach. There are courses organised throughout Britain that cover the following elements:

- where the club fits into the national structure
- what the coach does
- how the coach behaves
- the coach's responsibility
- how to screen new students
- the whys and wherefores of warm-up and cool-down
- training safety
- how to coach
- what insurance does and does not cover
- how to deal with emergencies.

An intermediate coaching award

For those coaches who want to further improve their coaching abilities, for example to run their own clubs, a third level of coaching accreditation is available. Again, there are courses run regularly around Great Britain that cover the following topics:

- how to get the best from students (the teaching of skills)
- how to measure their abilities (fitness)
- how to improve their performance (fitness)
- how to counsel students over training set-backs
- how to coach children and young students
- working with specific groups and injured students
- how to set targets and plan training
- opening, promoting and developing a club
- managing the club
- organising courses and events.

An advanced coaching award

For those coaches who aspire to the highest levels of coaching, there is a course specifically for them that covers the following units:

- the philosophy of coaching the martial arts
- the development of technical excellence
- the development of mobility
- the development of strength
- the development of speed
- the development of endurance
- the biomechanical analysis of technique
- nutrition
- factors affecting performance
- planning the programme.

This course is organised closely with a specific governing body, to facilitate an evaluation of the candidate's personal technical competence; assessment and grading skills; teaching of advanced techniques; and preparation of students for grading or competition.

With each of the four levels of coaching there will be a period of recording training sessions and lessons (lesson planning and recording are fully dealt with on page 70). These lessons will be monitored and a final evaluation of the coach's competence will be made.

The exact content and direction of the various levels of courses organised by governing bodies may vary from the format suggested here. However, any courses and levels of coaching competence cover all of the topics identified, though the emphasis might vary, as they are the essential elements of good coaching, irrespective of style.

For details of specific governing-body coaching awards, interested individuals should contact the appropriate organisation. Requirements of governing bodies may vary from style to style, and are constantly being reviewed with respect to current trends in technical development, sports science and legislation. It is therefore essential that aspiring coaches make themselves fully aware of current requirements and practices appropriate to their particular style.

Benefits of the programme

There are some very obvious benefits to be obtained from the implementation of a national coaching structure.

- It offers one nationally and internationally recognised set of awards for all of the martial arts.
- The levels of coaching competence are comparable with all governing bodies and associations.
- The structure of the awards and course content recognise the level of personal technical competence and involvement in a coach's particular style.
- The structure of the level of awards is linked closely to the individual governing body's and association's own levels of technical competence, experience and ability.
- The structure offers a clear pathway to coaching and developing a coaching hierarchy.

5

Martial arts: a way of life

For many students of martial arts it is the myth, legend and history of their particular style that attracts them, as well as the opportunity to learn the fighting skills. Indeed, with some students the philosophical aspects of their martial art are just as important, if not more so, than the physical ones. Most martial-arts students read widely about the history of the country from which their particular style came, along with studying the politics, economy, art, music and general culture that produced it. With this background such students have a unique approach to their involvement in their chosen style when compared to most other sportsmen and women.

However, the mystical or physical reasoning behind a student's interest in martial arts is moderated by the reality of his particular lifestyle. The martial artist's environment at home, school or work, plus his relationships with friends, emotional liaisons and financial status – amongst other factors – influence his attitudes, ambitions and willingness to endure the demands of training, grading and competition. You, the coach, must be ever sensitive to the changing environment in which a student lives and the manner in which it affects his involvement within the martial arts.

A supportive environment can produce a platform for any student to achieve success, no matter what he identifies the martial arts being able to offer him:

- a philosophy
- a way of life
- the development of self-confidence
- the development of discipline
- the chance to meet people and develop interpersonal skills
- the development of physical fitness
- the opportunity to learn complex skills
- personal development (grading)
- competition
- enjoyment.

The student has to identify that particular aspect of martial arts that, at

Though fighting skills obviously improve with training, the student can also achieve great personal development as well

least initially, attracts him to the activity. Obviously you should be equally aware of each and every student's aspirations such that you can create the best learning and teaching environment.

Society in general and the student's immediate family have a profound influence on him. Commitment, attitude, loyalty and responsibility are initially a result of the student's own experience, but they are markedly affected by the demands of each martial art or style. Basic requirements such as adequate hygiene, nutrition, sleep and a loving environment, which may not be at the top of your list of priorities, affect a student's performance. The lack of such basic needs can result not only in a loss of performance but, more importantly, in injury, disease and long-term personal and sporting deterioration.

The circle of friends in which a student moves has a profound effect upon his attitude towards martial arts. Their attitude towards society in general and the values of martial arts in particular influence the student. General social behaviour, drinking, smoking and relationships all have a bearing on how the student reacts to the demanding regime of martial-arts training and the degree of success that he achieves.

The immediate community in which a martial art operates is a major influence on performance. This is reflected in the facilities for training, ease of access and times of availability and the goodwill of the facility providers. The appropriate medical back-up with respect to doctors, physiotherapists and sports medicine and scientists in general should be available. Similarly, each student should receive personal attention no matter how brief, at every lesson. Each and every student is worthy of time from his coach, instructor or teacher. The aware coach provides effective, efficient and safe coaching, always makes immediate evaluation, and ensures that even the most demanding training is acceptable and even enjoyable.

6

The influence of age on learning

One of the problems when one studies the teaching of the many martial arts is that by and large they were developed by men for men at the peak of their physical condition for the battlefield or combat situation (see Fig. 4). However, recent research indicates that over 60% of all martial artists are under 16 years of age. Though it is true that some martial arts such as tai chi chuan tend to attract the more 'mature' students, others such as karate attract up to 75% juniors under 16 years of age. Within these statistics there is a clear dilemma for the martial arts!

It is perhaps true to suggest that most physical activities pride themselves on excellence of performance as identified by the skills of the participants or their success in competition. However, as has been shown, the peak of physical performance occurs during the mid-20s, which tends to indicate that only a small proportion of students will be 'successful' in the eyes of the general public and perhaps the governing body. It is often the case that national sports governing bodies gain status and recognition, often financial, because of their international competitive success.

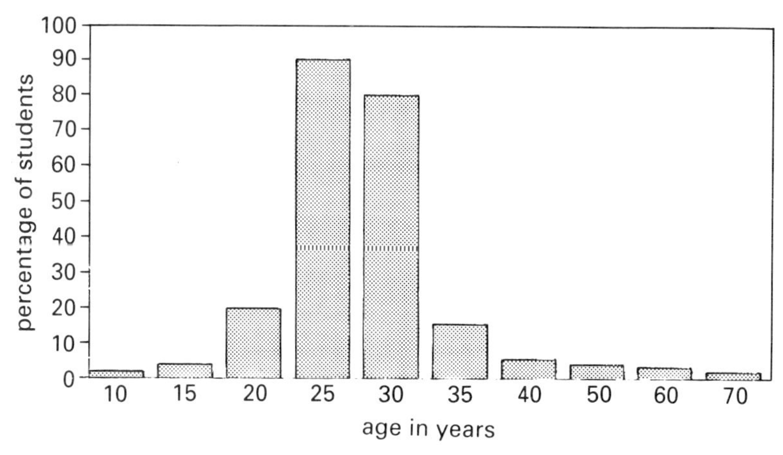

Fig. 4 Sporting success and age: if the age at which sportsmen and women achieve the peak of performance is analysed, most are successful in the 25 to 30 years range

By and large, martial arts techniques were devised by men for men at the peak of their physical and mental powers. However, there are many groups of students for whom particular consideration about the relevance of such techniques must be given; for example, over 60% of all students are under 16 years of age

However, how does one evaluate the quality of personal development and quality of coaching for those students who are either too young or too old to be 'successful' or are not involved in competitions? There is a further very important question to be considered. Is the teaching and learning environment the same for students of different ages? If it is not, what are the differences, and how might you utilise such information in your teaching?

There seem to be three broad age ranges to consider: juniors from 6 to 16, seniors from 16 to 30, and seniors over 30.

The young student

Recent studies have identified that in most sports and leisure activities in general, and the martial arts specifically, programmes to develop adults' fitness and skill are simply watered down to the limitations of youngsters. It is quite obvious that a seven-year-old student cannot perform to the same technical levels or generate as much force as a 30-year-old. How appropriate are adult training practices for juniors? I would suggest that they are not at all suitable. These studies, however, have also indicated a general pattern of motor and specific skill learning that is invaluable to a coach designing his work schedules for his junior students. This is especially so when it is realised that there is an almost parallel growth of physiological and psychological elements in the youngster, both of which are interwoven in any general or specific physical movement or technique, Fig. 5. It therefore follows that there has to be a carefully designed programme of martial-arts technique and skill learning that corresponds to the developmental level of the individual.

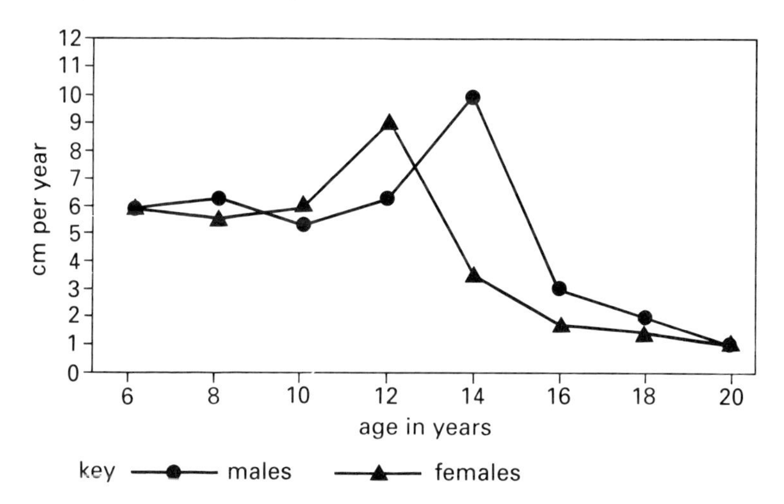

Fig. 5 Skeletal growth: hormonal influences bring about a rapid increase in height and body mass for girls between 11 and 13 and for boys between 13 and 15 years of age; brain function is also affected in the same periods

Development of motor learning

There is evidence to support the notion of four broad areas of motor learning, with respect to age (see Fig. 6).

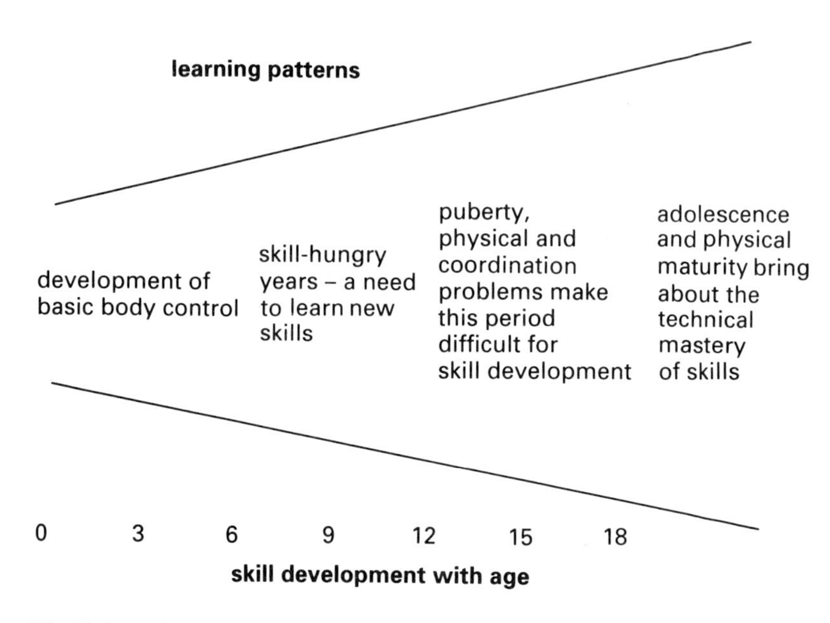

Fig. 6 Learning patterns: there is a sequential and progressive development of physical skills

Birth to two years

From birth and, according to some experts, before, the individual is evolving basic reflex-type movements. These tend to be basic postural movements, particularly those using the head, neck and back. The young child also experiments with the ability to move limbs by flexing and extending joints. Generally the infant is exploring his body and his ability to interact with his immediate surroundings. As sight, hearing, touch and balance improve, along with general physical and intellectual maturation, more demanding skills are performed such as sitting, reaching and grasping, crawling, standing and walking. These more advanced skills allow the infant to experience more stimuli from the world around him and create the foundation of intellectual and physical growth. This level of development is attained by the time the individual is about two years old. However, to stick rigidly to chronological age can be misleading because, as in all things, some youngsters improve at a rapid rate while others do not. But, generally speaking, by the age of two this level of attainment can be expected.

Two to eight years

As speech develops so too does the ability of the infant to communicate with the world in general. He is able to talk to others and express likes, dislikes and ideas. Furthermore, he is able to listen to new ideas and absorb information as part of the learning process. Walking progresses into running, while the development of judgement allows for variations in speed. Jumping and landing skills improve, as does their application into turning, bending, stretching, twisting, pushing and pulling activities. The individual becomes more aware of his body and how it moves and is able to coordinate its function and that of more intellectual reasoning in play and games. More complex skills that depend upon the integration of mind and body in a highly coordinated fashion evolve, for example throwing, punching, patting and kicking, along with catching and evasion techniques. These fundamental patterns of movement and perceptual-awareness aspects are generally established by the age of eight.

Eight to twelve years

From the age of eight these movement patterns can now be expanded and refined, mainly because the individual is aware of the position of his body or the 'feel' of a movement that allows him to modify the action as required. Also, very importantly, the youngster can now intellectually appreciate the quality of movement and understand what is needed. The skills learned in the previous stages act as the foundation for the new and specific ones introduced from now on. General patterns of movement are applied to specific activities and games. This level of development is generally attained by the age of 12.

Twelve to sixteen years

From the ages of 12 to 16 the application of skills develops, as do the intellectual and reasoning powers. There tends to be much more specialisation than before into specific sports or activities in which the interest of the individual lies. With the onset of puberty and adulthood, there is a great change, not only in the physical make-up of the youngster but also in a whole series of behavioural, emotional, sociological and intellectual ways. Physical activity becomes more important as exercise and as leisure and recreation. Other values such as competition, social interaction, attainment, making friends and many more begin to be formed.

The sequence of these developmental stages is progressive in that the skills learned in one phase are the foundation for refinement into more complex ones in the next. It is very difficult, if not impossible, to teach any individual a skill or technique appropriate to his developmental stage if he has not experienced, let alone mastered, the previous ones.

The evolution of skills

The evolution of skills seems to follow a progressive pattern in chronological order, along the following lines.

The first stage

The infant has an awareness of:

- being alive
- his body, limbs and movement
- his physical situation and place with respect to the world
- up, down, left, right and combinations of direction
- time – present, future and past
- tempo and rhythm
- coordinating hand and foot movements to vision.

There is also general development of the senses (vision, hearing, touch, balance, smell and taste).

The second stage

As the basic senses improve and the body begins to grow, these elements can be incorporated into the refinement of slightly more complex skills: reaching, grasping, sitting, crawling, standing, falling, walking, running with variations of pace and style, jumping with variations in take-off, landing with variations of feet positions, rolling and climbing.

The third stage

As these movement skills develop, there is a need for greater intellectual interaction, particularly with selection of the correct movement pattern appropriate to the individual's response to a given situation. He develops whole-body movements: pushing, pulling, spinning, twisting, bending and stretching.

The fourth stage

These whole-body movements provide once again a platform for the more complex skills that require the coordination of the whole body with specific and fine movements of particular parts: throwing, punching, patting, bouncing, kicking, catching and trapping with the feet.

Junior students are not 'little adults'; they are vulnerable to excessive physical and psychological pressures. Training for them can and should be fun!

Coaching considerations

You, the martial-arts coach, face a fundamental problem from the outset. Techniques used in martial arts were designed mainly by men, for use by men in the conflict situation. These techniques presuppose that individuals have a measure of strength, speed, endurance and mobility as a basis on which such skills can be learned. It does not require much insight to assume that youngsters do not have these elements of fitness to the same degree as an adult. Furthermore, there is a more basic problem. How can you hope to teach to a seven-year-old complex techniques, let alone their application – which requires a high level of intellectual maturity – when he is only just developing the elemental skills of learning how to use his body in a coordinated fashion? Before any complex skills can be taught, the foundation elements of basic body movements have to be established. Simplistically, a child who cannot throw or catch a ball is going to have difficulty with the much more complex techniques involved in punching and blocking and their variations.

There is another very important physiological factor that has to be clearly understood by you. Junior students are very vulnerable to intensive training: immature bones and joints, ligaments, tendons and muscles can be damaged irreparably. These injuries can remain with them for the rest of their lives. You must be aware of their limitations and plan the programme accordingly. The poor function of other important immature body systems such as the cardio-vascular system and digestion can affect the various energy systems. Young students tend to work better at low work levels; they seem to go on for ever. Intensive work occurs in short bursts with periods of rest between; attention span and concentration seem to operate in a similar way.

There is an equally important psychological element too. Juniors are developing their intellectual and emotional skills. They are very vulnerable to the pressures placed on them by over-enthusiastic parents and coaches. It is important that those responsible do not become carried away with the successes or defeats of their charges. Juniors have difficulty in handling victory or despair; they need the support of those around them. It is essential that this large group of students is nurtured in the proper way to encourage their long-term participation in the martial arts.

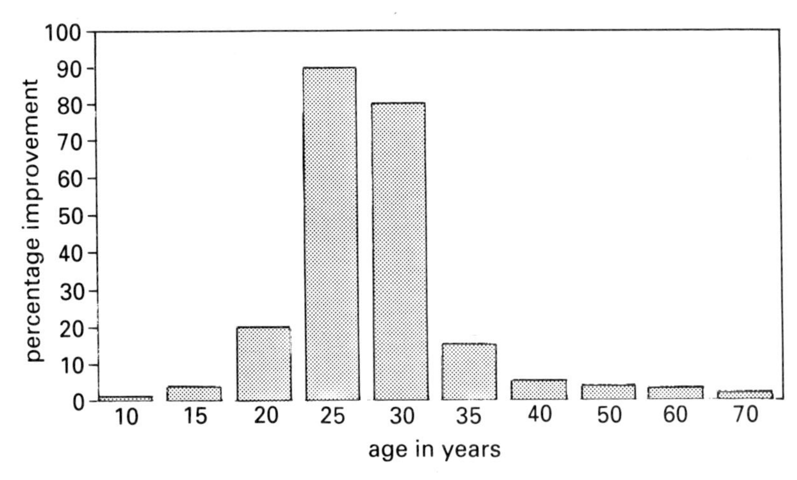

Fig. 7 Physical potential and age: an individual attains the peak of his potential for excellence in physical activity between 25 and 30 years of age

Sixteen to thirty years

From 16 years on all of the psychological, social and corresponding emotional processes continue to mature, along with all of the physiological systems. The psychological and physical elements needed to produce excellence in the components of fitness (speed, strength, stamina, suppleness and skill) continue to develop towards their peak at approximately 25 (see Fig. 7).

It is during this period (16 to 30 years) that students are best suited to achieving their potential. They are mentally and physically able to withstand the demands of training, grading and competition. However, it is a fact that only a small proportion of students stay in the martial arts long enough to be able to fully exploit this period in their lives and reach their peak of performance.

Thirty years and older

From the age of 30, various physical and intellectual functions begin to decline. Fortunately they do not all decline at the same rate, and there are great variations between individuals in the rates of degeneration, Fig 8.

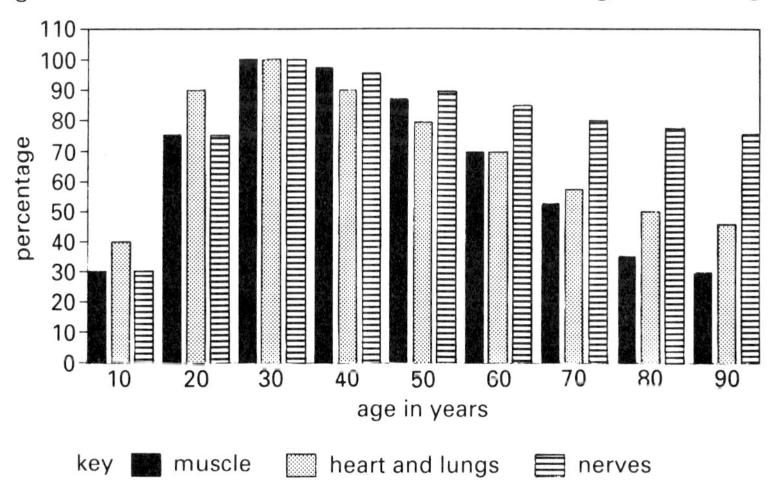

Fig. 8 Decline in physical function: not all of the body's systems decline at the same rate with increased age

The ageing process

The main systems involved in the ageing process that have an effect on martial arts training are as follows.

The skeletal system

This is composed in the main of calcium. With age there is less calcium laid down in the bones, which can lead to thinner and potentially more brittle bones (see Figs. 9, 10) predominant in post-menopausal women. Obviously training loads should be modified to reduce the burden on the skeletal system. With age, joints begin to lose their natural lubricant and

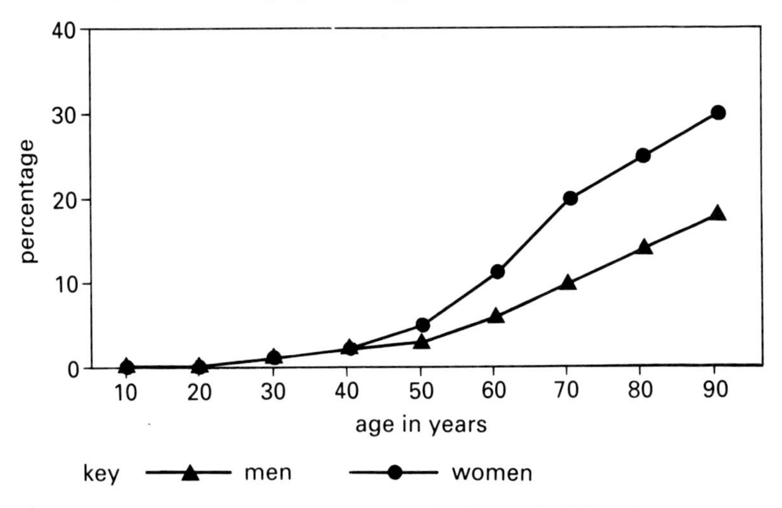

Fig. 9 Bone loss: with age there is a gradual loss of calcium from bone tissue

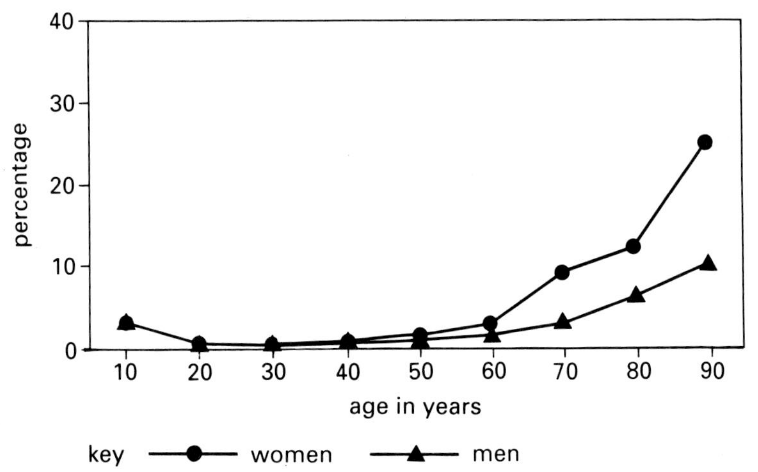

Fig. 10 Age-related fractures: as bone loss continues, there is an associated increase in fractures

become stiffer. There can be inflammation of joints or structural degeneration. Obviously in both instances the range of movement that a mature student can achieve gradually diminishes.

Muscles

Muscles begin to lose their size and consequently their strength. Those specialised fibres involved in producing fast movements are generally the first to be affected. With age, therefore, strength gradually decreases and speed reduces much faster. Where strength, speed or power are an intrinsic element of training, older students are at a disadvantage, Fig. 11. Muscles and other connective tissues such as ligaments and tendons lose their elasticity with age, and this loss has a major effect on any force that they can generate and the range of movement involved.

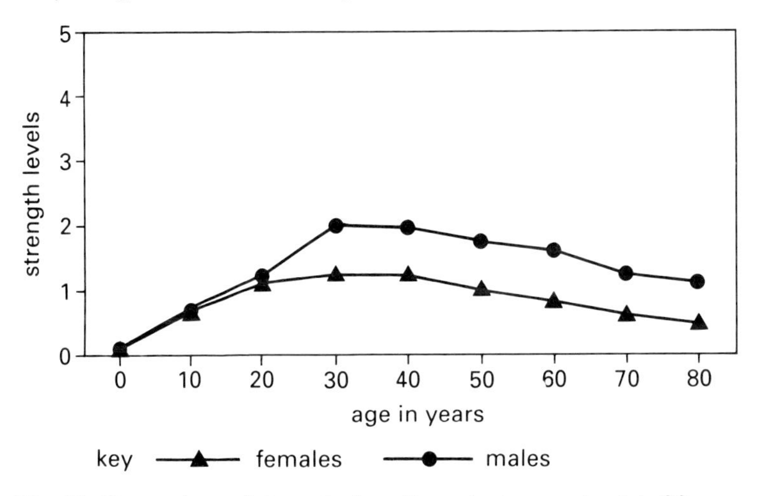

Fig. 11 Comparison of strength: from its peak at approximately 30 years of age, this gradually declines with age

The nervous systems

The nervous systems go through two main degenerative processes. Firstly, the total number of nerves can decline by as much as 37%. Secondly, the speed at which nerves transmit information can deteriorate by over 10%. This latter loss of function markedly affects the rate at which information is sent to the brain and processed to produce the required response in either a major organ or muscle group. Skills and reaction times become slower in execution but not less accurate (see Fig. 12).

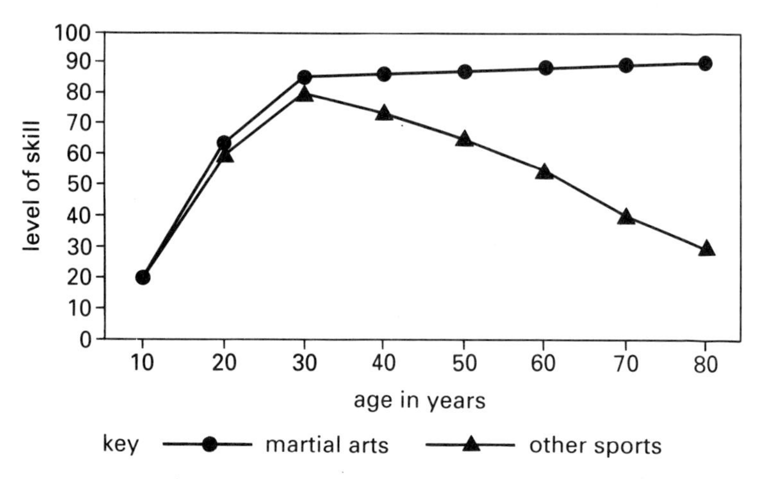

Fig. 12 Martial-arts training and age: though physical function might decline, the level of skill can continue to improve with age

Attention, concentration span and memory function can also be adversely affected.

The cardio-vascular system

The cardio-vascular system involves the coordinated efforts of the heart to pump blood that has been enriched with oxygen in the lungs through the arteries to reach all parts of the body. The abundance or lack of oxygen in active tissues affects the work rate of a student.

With age, heart rate declines gradually (see Fig. 13). There is a formula used in some training methods that illustrates the relationship between age and heart rate: maximum heart rate (beats per minute) = 220 – age (years). For example, let's compare the maximum heart rate for a 30- and 60-year-old student, both male. + 30-year-old maximum heart rate = 220 – 30 = 190. + 60-year-old maximum heart rate = 220 – 60 = 160. Be careful with heart rates as indicators of fitness, especially when comparing males and females. On average, at any age a female's heart beats eight beats per minute faster than that of a male of the same age and fitness level (see Fig. 14).

The function of the lungs in absorbing oxygen from the air, while at the same time getting rid of carbon dioxide, also deteriorates with the passing of the years. The volume and elasticity of lung tissue decreases, thereby reducing the total volume of oxygen and carbon dioxide being processed.

The elasticity of the blood vessels declines with age. At the same time

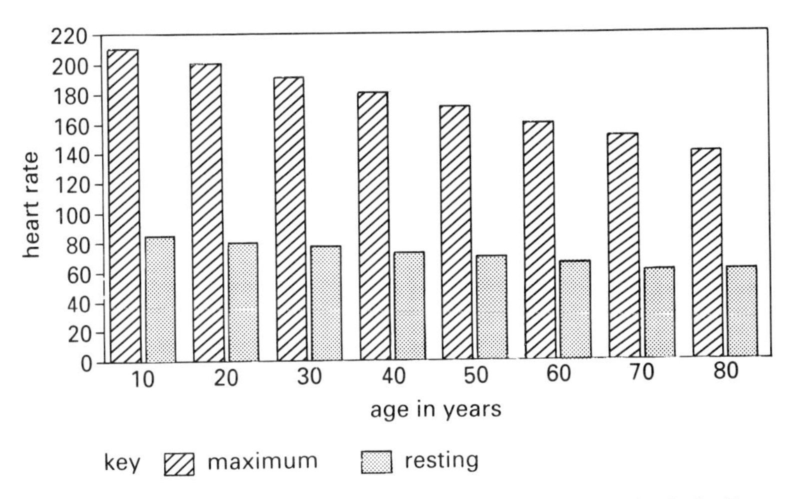

Fig. 13 Heart rate and age: maximum and resting heart rates both decline with age

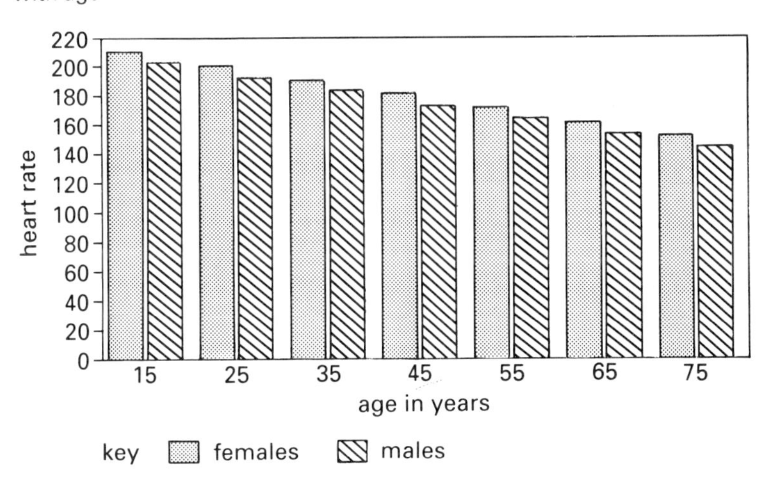

Fig. 14 Maximum heart rate and age: the heart rate of females is higher than that of comparable males of the same age and level of fitness

there is a gradual constriction of the major arteries caused by a build-up of fatty deposits. Both of these factors reduce the flow of blood through vessels.

The cumulative effect of reducing heart rate, lung function and blood flow markedly reduces oxygen availability in active tissue, thereby reducing a student's work rate. The efficiency of the brain in all its aspects is also affected as it requires abundant supplies of oxygen to operate properly (see Fig. 15).

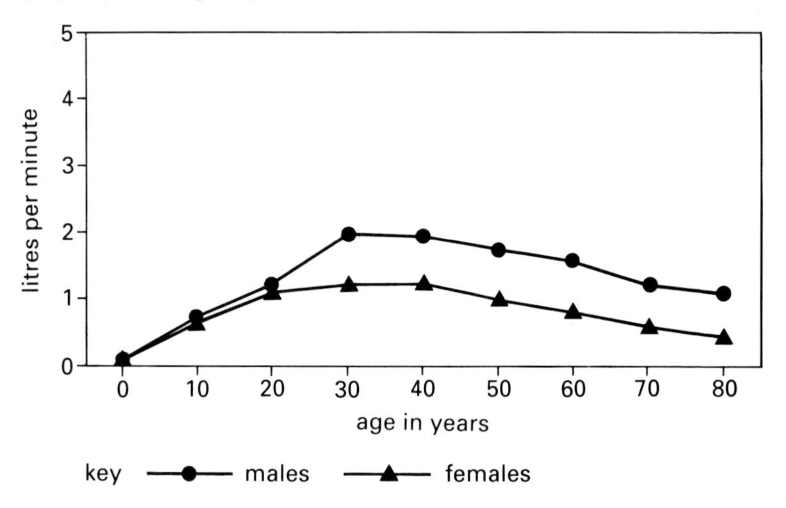

Fig. 15 Maximum oxygen consumption: the body's abiliy to extract oxygen from the atmosphere and use it to provide energy for physical activity declines with age

Other body functions

There is associated loss of performance with other major body functions and organs such as digestion, which provides the energy for training and the consequent removal of body waste. Though very important, they are not as important in the skill-learning environment as the other factors mentioned.

Body composition

One of the insidious aspects of ageing is that there is a gradual change in body composition. As lean body mass decreases, there is a corresponding increase in the depositing of body fat, see Fig. 16. This increase in body weight, which is of no benefit to performance at all, also puts increased strain on the less efficient skeletal, muscular, cardio-vascular and other body systems. Again, in the training programme this factor must be considered.

Coaches and students should, however, not lose heart about the inevitable loss in body function with age. There is good news! Most medical sources confirm the fact that a programme of regular physical activity, and it does not have to be intensive or strenuous, reduces the rate of degeneration. Not only is the ageing process retarded, general health and well-being also continue, because of the maintained function of vital organs.

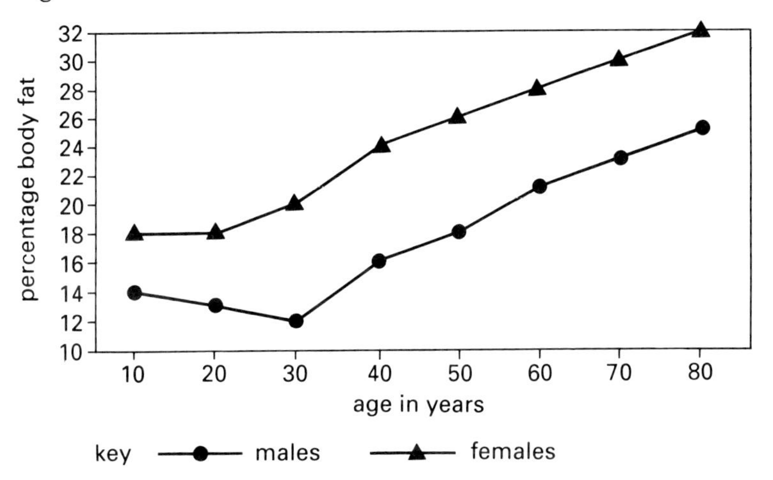

Fig. 16 Body composition and age: lean body mass decreases with age

Technical improvement and age

It has been demonstrated that the optimum time for improvement in training is the period from 16 to 30 years. Improvement can occur at all ages but the potential for any increase in performance declines with age (see Fig. 17). You must be aware of the ageing process when designing

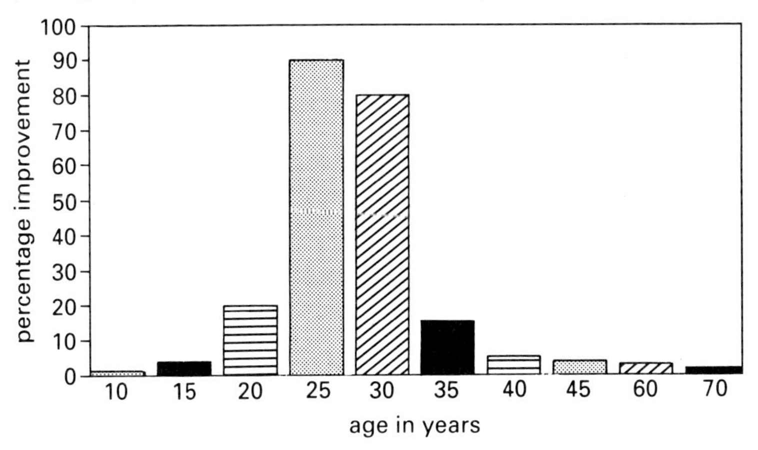

Fig. 17 Improvement and age: the potential for improvement in performance declines with age

lessons that are specifically for or have mature students in them. You must be aware of their limitations in training and potential for improvement.

Practical considerations

One of the characteristics of most martial-arts clubs is the mixed age, gender and ability of students in the same class. As we have seen in this section, work for a 25-year-old is different to that for an 8-year-old or 60-year-old. The problem is not just in levels of fitness; it is far more fundamental. There are major physiological factors that have to be taken into account and, more importantly, the potential for learning and improvement is also very different.

Some clubs organise their classes so that juniors learn separately from the seniors. Perhaps there is an argument for three groups. The ages indicated are only a suggestion; you might want to vary them slightly but still cover the three broad groups.

- Group 1: under-16-year-olds? They develop all of the basic movement skills, as identified, and having mastered them begin to learn the less demanding martial-arts skills.
- Group 2: 16- to 30-year-olds? They are in a position to develop their physical condition and level of skill to the highest possible standard.
- Group 3: 30 years and older? They put more emphasis on the technical, philosophical and spiritual – and not the physical – elements.

Obviously this is an ideal situation that has to be tempered by reality. But I am sure that you understand the thinking behind the groupings. Such a structure also allows for those students who have different expectations from the various styles to join the appropriate group. With this strategy the age-related learning patterns and physical constraints can be monitored more easily than with a fully integrated class.

The development of martial-arts skills

The improvement and refinement of martial-arts skills does not take place overnight. Many years of dedication to a particular style are necessary to achieve excellence. In many sports and leisure pursuits a working grasp of the activity can be quickly achieved by the participants. This is not the case with the martial arts as, by their very complexity, any competence or success takes a long time to achieve. Perhaps this is the reason for a high percentage of drop-outs early on in the training process. If students are seeking a rapid rate of improvement, they are going to be quickly disillusioned and stop training. Perhaps this also explains the commitment, dedication and loyalty of those martial artists who have been able to endure the psychological and physical rigours of training over several years to achieve their desired level of competence.

In most sporting activities the participants reach the optimum age for success around 26. Though this may also hold true of the martial arts as well, there is an extra element that has to be considered. Initially, the learning of fighting techniques is simple: the development of physical skills. As they are refined to a very high degree, their relevance and application become more important. There is a shift in training from knowledge of skills to an understanding of their purpose and development. Though the physical aspect of training is still important, there is more of an emphasis on the individual and his philosophical outlook and self-evaluation as to his involvement in the whole structure of his particular style. For many students this is when they begin to develop an understanding as to the real meaning of that style. The truly competent martial artist, as identified by the traditionalists, is the student who has realised that though the development of physical, mental and technical skills is important, the overriding essential element is overall knowledge and understanding of the art. What this means in practice is that though the physical powers of a student may begin to decline with age, his increased awareness and perception of his style allow him to continue to improve his overall performance and level of competence as long as he continues to train, Fig. 18.

It is a simple fact that students can continue to improve throughout their life, which gives the martial arts the edge on most, if not all, other

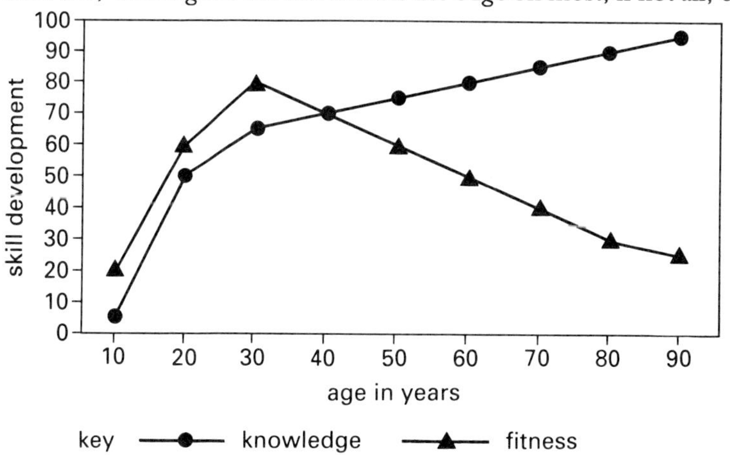

Fig. 18 Martial-arts skill and age: though fitness may decline with age, knowledge, understanding and technical competence continue to improve

The martial arts offer youngsters the opportunity to develop basic movement skills at the same time as developing their personality and character

sports and leisure activities. Too often the general public and students just see the execution of devastatingly effective technique as being the be-all and end-all of training. This is far from the truth. There are no other physical activities that can offer enjoyable physical exercise that can develop youngsters' basic movement skills, while at the same time developing their personality and character. So, in adolescence and maturity, when competition is important to some students, the martial arts caters for them, while for students reaching maturity and old age, the perfection of technique in its purest form is possible because little in the way of physical effort is required.

Those students who want to follow their own direction in competition, those who look for personal development through grading and training, and those who seek the aesthetic and discipline of kata or form work can all be catered for at any age, any level of ability and any level of commitment. Which other sports or physical activities can take their sportsmen and women from the cradle to the grave? It is time that all practitioners began to promote this unique aspect of the martial arts. In this way the general public might be made more aware of the contribution of the martial arts to the physical, personal, sporting and general development of all of their participants.

It is unfortunate that the general impression that the person in the street has of the various fighting styles is a caricature of reality. Films and videos that emphasise the 'deadly' power that 'experts' in martial arts possess do little to enhance the status of the various styles. Whereas it might be true that Bruce Lee, Chuck Norris, the 'Karate Kid' and the 'Mutant Ninja Turtles' have done much to create an interest in a certain aspect of what might loosely be called 'fighting skills', they have done very little to promote the underlying principles of most styles as identified by Master Funakoshi Gichin.

7

The role of the senses in the learning process

The five senses that he possesses are the means by which any student identifies the requirements or demands of any new technique. The degree to which each of the senses contributes to the learning process has been approximated as follows: vision 75%, hearing 13%, touch 6%, taste 3% and smell 3%, while balance is an essential element of any if not all skills and is a combination of the above and specialised sensors in the ears.

The function of all of the senses is to allow the student to create a mental image of the pattern of movement that you are trying to teach. The most difficult part of the learning and teaching process is to create in the student's mind the image of the technical excellence of a movement that you have in yours. For it is the exemplar of excellence that you bring to mind that you are trying to place in the mind of each and every student. It is therefore essential in both the learning and teaching processes that the optimum conditions are created.

Vision

Traditionally martial arts are taught in rows; however, there are certain limitations that have to be identified with this type of class organisation. Students in the back rows may not see clearly the technique being demonstrated or taught, because of the bodies in the way. Obviously students at the back who are small or have any visual defects are severely disadvantaged. Perhaps equally importantly, but not fully appreciated, is that *every* student, no matter which row he is in, sees the demonstration from a slightly different angle. The 'interpretation' of the technique that each student sees is slightly different, which might account for any discrepancy in performance. Any student can only reproduce the movement pattern that he sees. If his vision is impaired or the view that he has is not perfect, then the image of the movement that he perceives is slightly, but possibly significantly, different to the one that you intend. It is essential that any demonstration is clearly visible to each student and that anyone with a visual defect positions himself close to you.

Students acquire over 75% of the information that they need to understand a technique through their eyes. Demonstrations should therefore be organised so that not only can all of the students see the technique but also that the pattern of movement required is clearly and accurately identified

Vision and hearing

The importance of a technically correct demonstration is obviously critical in the learning process of any student. It does not follow that this must be performed by you; a senior student demonstrating would be equally effective. However, with modern technology the use of videotapes, films, photographs, wall charts and many other visual sources illustrating élite performers can be very helpful in the hands of an experienced coach. They can in some instances be more effective than a demonstration by you, in that they can allow for verbal instruction, identifying essential aspects of technique and performance, to accompany the visual input. As previously stated, hearing accounts for 13% of the total sensory appreciation of a technique. This can be made even more valuable if the verbal description or commentary accompanies the demonstration. In this way the various points that the student should note are identified during the movement, which makes them more obvious.

Hearing

There is another aspect to the contribution of hearing to the learning environment that follows very closely that of vision. In the classic rows of martial-arts training, students at the back of the class or any who have a hearing disability are not able to hear fully or accurately what is required of them. It stands to reason that if a student misunderstands instructions or comments, the way he performs a technique or action is different to what you expect. It is essential therefore that clear and precise instructions are given by you; you must be able to project your voice and vary the tone so that every student in the group can hear precisely what is required. From an organisational point of view it is good practice for any student with a hearing difficulty to stand close to you.

Touch

Touch has a very important role to play in the learning of skills. Obviously when holding an opponent or a piece of equipment its value is self-evident: it identifies the degree and intensity of force as well as any grip that is necessary. Similarly it is essential for most, if not all, techniques that a constant feedback of information from the feet about the degree of grip that they have with the floor is available for the student. If he is likely to slip or has sound footing, the choice of techniques to be used is affected. In groundwork, important sensory information from various parts of the body is constantly being monitored.

Kinaesthesis

Under the umbrella of all of the senses in general and the nervous system in particular lies perhaps one of the most important senses, that of 'kinaesthesis'. In muscles and joints there are sensory nerves that provide a constant stream of data for the brain. This information gives details of the state of contraction and therefore the length of a muscle and the amount of force that it is generating. This knowledge, together with information about the angle at joints, gives the brain the details as to what exactly limbs and joints are doing and their positions. Other internal organs, particularly those involved with balance, also provide an invaluable input.

In this way the student is conscious of what the various parts of his body are doing while he is performing a technique. It is essential that he learns what the signals associated with the correct movement pattern are. In this way he can 'feel' when he has performed a technique correctly or incorrectly. You must appreciate that it is this feedback from the muscles and joints that is stored in the brain as the technique. It is that pattern of movement as identified by the various sensory organs that is reproduced when that particular action is required.

How many times have you said to a student learning a technique, 'Can't you feel what you are doing?' Alternatively, when a student is erratic in the quality of performance, you might ask, 'Are you able to feel the difference between when it's right and when it's wrong?' It is the kinaesthetic sense, the ability of a student to appreciate what muscles, joints and limbs are doing and their position, that you are referring to.

Taste and smell

The senses of taste and smell may not rapidly spring to mind as being vital avenues of learning! There has been recent research that suggests that both are perhaps more important in providing information than one might suspect. From various parts of the body, waste products and general body secretions are produced. Even with the most fastidious cleanliness, they still occur. Perhaps one of the less obvious of these sources of waste 'removal' is perspiration. In times of extreme stress and illness the nature of these products is imperceptibly changed.

It is widely accepted that many species in the animal kingdom can sense or 'smell' fear; it is the human senses of taste and smell, which in several ways are very similar, that detect waste products. These body secretions in humans are generally detected at two levels, the conscious and the subconscious ones. Apart from the very obvious information that the nose or the taste buds detect, it is now thought that very subtle information is detected and processed at a subconscious level. This data is then added to the overall availability of information from which we make decisions, perhaps about a person's character or attitude. For example: 'He is timid'; 'He is aggressive'; or 'I like my teacher'. Perhaps our own emotional perceptions about a person – such as love, hate and fear – are provided with information by these two senses.

The full picture of the contribution of the various senses to the learning environment is far from clear. What is apparent is that all of them make a very positive contribution to the efficiency of learning. Any learning or teaching environment, if it is to be effective, must make use of all of the means of providing information. The mechanism by which knowledge is acquired by the student is the senses. It is for you to ensure that any new skill or information is presented in such a way that the sensitivity of any or all of the senses can be fully exploited.

8

The role of the coach

To be a coach in any sport is a great honour. For parents to entrust their children to your care indicates their belief in you as a respectable and honourable person. Furthermore, to be able to control the sporting destinies of all of your students is a privilege. However, with such a position of trust, there is a great deal of responsibility to maintain both personal and coaching standards. Your duties are wide ranging and personally demanding (see Fig. 19). It is vital that anyone considering taking up the challenge of becoming a coach is aware of the full extent of the requirements.

It may seem simplistic, but it is nevertheless true that, 'you can be a martial-arts student without a coach but you cannot be a coach without students'. You offer a service. If it is what prospective students can relate to and enjoy, you will be successful. If, however, you present your martial art in such a way that it cannot be appreciated by others, you will be unsuccessful. A recent survey suggested that élite and successful com-

your coaching duties	other responsibilities
instructor	knowledge
teacher	enthusiasm
trainer	safety
motivator	discipline
disciplinarian	maturity
social worker	willingness
friend	respect
scientist	fairness
student	coolness
manager	recognition
administrator	support
publicity agent	good samaritan

Fig. 19 The role of the coach: the duties and responsibilities of the coach are far-ranging and demanding

petitive martial artists at international level were highly unsuccessful when it came to running their own clubs. They simply could not present the activity in a way that could be appreciated and enjoyed by 'lesser mortals'. You therefore have to arrive at a compromise, at least with novices, in that you must offer the students a package that they can relate to but that does not offend your ideals or the underpinning philosophy of the martial art.

Technical standards

The very nature of the martial arts requires anyone who desires to be a coach to have a very high personal standard of technical competence. The only way that the multitude of martial-arts skills can be taught in safety is by an experienced practitioner. You have to be able to demonstrate the techniques, explain their application and create a safe training environment that allows students to learn and improve. Only an in-depth personal understanding of the requirements of the techniques allows this to happen. Again, if you require a high technical standard of your students, you must be able to demonstrate that quality of movement. You must, however, identify your limitations.

Not all students participate in the martial arts for the same reasons; each one of them enjoys or values a particular aspect. These might include: training, grading, competition, physical activity, friendship, discipline, religious undertones, philosophical aspects, responsibility and possibly many others. It is clear that when a student takes on the extra responsibility of coaching other students, it is only natural that he tends to emphasise those aspects that gave him the most satisfaction and pleasure. Obviously any bias in teaching is attractive to some students, as equally it is complete anathema to others. You must present a balanced programme of training that encompasses all elements of the martial arts. Obviously in areas where you have a particular expertise, it should be made available to the students.

Personal standards

Students learn in the first instance by copying the person who they see as epitomising all that is good in the martial arts. They see the coach as their 'hero' or role model. The students' attitudes, level of commitment, behaviour and personal values are based on those of their coach. You therefore have to be the exemplar of punctuality, good manners, dress, conduct and commitment. You must say 'Do as I do' and not 'Do as I say'. It must be appreciated that, whether you like it or not, you will produce 'clones'! They will mimic not only skills as taught but also other mannerisms such as posture, nervous habits, attitudes and behaviour of their teacher that he might not like to have 'laid bare' to the public.

You have to be enthusiastic about the martial art, the individuals in the class and what you are teaching. You have to encourage the students to want to learn and to achieve the highest possible standard of performance. To help the students want to learn, you must establish a positive teaching style: not too authoritarian and yet not too *laissez-faire*. A sense of humour is vital in the creation of an enjoyable learning environment that produces happy students who are positively motivated to work well.

Communication skills

One of the historical traditions of the martial arts was that when a student attained a certain level of technical competence, it was automatically assumed that he could now teach. As previously mentioned, there is a subtle flaw in this logic. No matter how skilful a student may be, it does not mean that he has the ability to pass his knowledge and skills on to others. There was another negative traditional practice, which was that of not giving the student any information as to how well he was doing. There has to be constant feedback from coach to student, identifying good points of technique and any errors. Furthermore, you have to identify to the student how any faults can be rectified. But simple encouragement by you of the student's efforts can be one of the most valuable contributions to the development of his skills and understanding.

There is a very obvious outlet for your communication skills, which to some may not be immediately apparent, that of publicity. For any club to be successful it must have good coverage in the local media, be it in the press, on radio or on T.V. By regularly featuring in the news, not only does the club publicise the efforts of its current members, but it also builds up a good name, which is in itself a great recruitment asset. However, you have to monitor what information is released to the media and, if necessary, identify personnel or resources to facilitate such coverage.

Interpersonal skills

Coaches do not teach martial-arts techniques, they teach students, people! In order to be able to motivate each student, you have to be able to understand and relate to them. There has to exist a strong coach–student relationship if the learning and teaching environment is to be effective. You have to be able to communicate with each student at a level that he understands. Furthermore, he must be able to develop both an interest in and positive attitude to training in general and the martial art in particular. You must be able to capture the mind of the student and fire his enthusiasm to want to learn more.

Management skills

In order to create an effective and safe learning environment, you must be able to organise your students and lesson well. In all martial arts there is a possibility of accidents through a variety of situations. It is essential therefore that there is a high level of discipline in the activities both of the class and each student. This discipline does not have to be overbearing to be effective. It is essential that in creating a safe and controlled environment, you can deal with students firmly but fairly and not show favour.

The organisation of the various students who you teach is of vital importance. Does the lesson require a class activity, or group, partner or individual practice? Being able to identify the structure of a practice is not quite the same as getting to work efficiently and effectively.

The coach who is in charge of a club or a group of other coaches may have to adopt more obvious management skills. He may have to identify the individual roles of the other staff and define any special responsibilities. With such a structure of delegation, the senior coach also has to create a procedure for assessing the effectiveness of his assistants.

Coaching a new club

In Britain a coach has usually trained as a student for a long period of time within a club and its affiliated governing body and association. With this practice a coach is very familiar with students and coaches of a particular club and the administrative protocol of the governing body. However, this situation may not always hold true; coaches do take over lessons or clubs without having had the benefit of a long-term association. If you are in such a situation it is imperative that you gather as much information as possible before taking up your coaching duties. It will be on the basis of such information that you plan the individual lessons and long-term training programme. If you are very familiar with a club, you must not be complacent and assume that you know all that you need when commencing your coaching duties. The following check-list might help in collecting all of the important information.

The preliminary visit

The aims are to:

- obtain any information and material required
- meet the existing coach and assistants
- meet the classes and individual students

Any activity must take place under the watchful eye of the coach. Without individual feedback and encouragement, training can become boring and counter-productive, as bad attitudes and poor technique may develop

- assess the atmosphere of the school, classes and learning environment
- assess the training facility and equipment
- note any possible problems with the facility providers or other users.

You should look for:

- the philosophy of the school, its tradition and training, grading and competition structure

- routine organisation
- training days and times
- existing style of coaching
- attitudes and expectations of students.

You should note:

- names of students in classes
- size of classes
- ages and abilities of students
- length of lessons
- equipment and apparatus
- facilities
- details of students with any special problems
- existing grading, competition or other fixtures.

The perceptive coach might have particular opinions and views as to his particular function within the club and identify other important elements worthy of consideration. It is for each coach to decide what he needs to know in order to carry out his coaching duties.

9

Planning training

The content of any lesson is only of any value if it is an integral and sequential part of a long-term programme. Lessons that are out of sequence or taught 'off the cuff' are not only of little value to the student, they also indicate a lack of forethought, planning and commitment on your part. With most martial arts there are fixed time periods and dates that have to be considered when looking at a long-term programme. Most styles have a set period between gradings, which may vary between three and twelve months, or even longer.

A programme of work is a survey of the work that you intend to cover over a period of time. It helps to provide continuity in the lessons and their progressive sequence in the learning process. The programme should include the who? why? and what? of coaching:

- who? details of the various students to be taught (their age, gender, potential and current standard)
- why? the general aims of the programme
- what? the techniques and activities to be taught; the number of lessons available; the programme broken down into weeks and individual lessons.

By setting down a skeletal programme of work, the caring coach can see not only which techniques are to be taught and when, but also how they follow each other sequentially. Furthermore, with such a plan for each grade within the class, you can devise individual lesson plans to ensure that all students benefit as much as possible from a lesson.

The long-term plan

You have to study carefully the syllabus that is appropriate to each grade within the class. Some governing bodies do not have even a 'minimum' syllabus. Once the techniques have been identified, you then have to include them in the appropriate lesson. When you have repeated this procedure for all of the grades, you will know exactly which techniques need to be taught in each lesson (see Figs 20, 21). This can be of great help in devising the individual lesson plan.

Period commencing												
Grade	wk 1	wk 2	wk 3	wk 4	wk 5	wk 6	wk 7	wk 8	wk 9	wk 10	wk 11	wk 12

Fig. 20 Planning the programme (short-term): the coach indicates the kyu grades, or similar, in the left-hand column; he then identifies which technique will be taught to a specific grade each week

Having identified all of the techniques that have to be taught each lesson, you can consider how you are going to teach them. For example, if there are five different grades in the class and all of them have to learn and develop a particular kick, punch, throw, block or lock, these techniques can be taught to the whole class. There may be techniques that are common to two grades and others that are relevant to the rest of the grades. Therefore you can teach two groups, each working on a common skill. If there are specific techniques that are different for each grade, the class can split into individual grade groups, working on techniques appropriate only to them.

This practice is not only appropriate for the teaching of a new skill, it is equally valid for the review and refinement of those already learned. The entire programme can be planned in this fashion, not only to identify what the overall programme of work is, but also how each lesson fits into that structure. Equally important is the fact that having such information to hand, you can quite easily construct a lesson plan.

The overall structure of a lesson plan is a dynamic one. Consider a novice student who is working on a twelve-week programme to grade to a higher level. In the early stages the lesson emphasises the warm-up and general introductory activities. The student may not be physically prepared for the specific demands of the techniques that need to be learned and perfected for the appropriate grading. Particular exercises may have to be included in the lesson to develop the specific 'S' factors (strength, speed, suppleness, stamina and skill) required for technical excellence. Novice students in particular have to be eased gently into the demands of martial-arts training. Initially therefore there may be much more of an emphasis than later on game and fun-type activities to create a desire to want to train and learn.

Aims of the training programme

When devising a teaching programme, you must clearly identify what you are expecting your students to learn. This ultimate purpose of involvement in the martial arts is usually described as the 'aim' of training. These aims are the 'ideal' purpose of training towards that which we may strive for but never reach. In the struggle to achieve the 'ideal', you have to identify more realistic, attainable targets. These can be useful indicators of the student's progression or level of achievement.

With any systematic and progressive long-term training regime, there has to be an underlying target or series of targets to be achieved. You have to decide which targets you feel are the most important. Is training designed to:

Month – Week commencing																								
Week training year	1	2	3	4	5	6	7	8	9	10	11	12	13	14	15	16	17	18	19	20	21	22	23	24

Planned competition/Grading programme		
Date	Venue	Competition/Grading

Fig. 21 Planning the programme (long-term): the coach again indicates the kyu grade in the left-hand column; he can repeat the process for the short-term programme, identifying the techniques to be taught for a grade each

25	26	27	28	29	30	31	32	33	34	35	36	37	38	39	40	41	42	43	44	45	46	47	48	49	50	51	52

Notes

week; he can also identify gradings, competitions and any other important dates

- bring about an increase in the number and quality of martial-arts skills?
- prepare a student for life?
- help a student to become a valuable member of society?
- develop in a student an appreciation of the cultural, moral, emotional, and spiritual heritage of his martial art in particular and humanity in general?

The following mnemonic 'M.A.R.T.I.A.L. A.R.T.' might be of use to you when attempting to identify some of the more important aspects of setting goals.

M Measure: you must measure any improvements in the quality of technical or personal standards.

A Action: you have to identify a specific target and a plan of action to achieve it.

R Realistic: you must set realistic targets that the student can attain.

T Training: a plan of action needs to be devised before training starts.

I Intermediate: intermediate training must be identified as attainable targets.

A Acceptance: students must accept the demands of the learning process.

L Learn: students need to be motivated to learn and improve.

A Application: students must apply themselves to the work programme.

R Responsibility: students must accept responsibility for their technical and personal standards.

T Time: the amount of training is proportional to improvement.

If all of the objectives of the training programme are M.A.R.T.I.A.L. A.R.T. ones, then there is more chance of success for both your students and your efforts. Obviously some of the elements are more easily measured than others, for example the number of press-ups. However, with the qualitative assessment of technical excellence there are difficulties.

When devising a training plan for a group or an individual student, it is important that the purpose of training is identified. Obviously you have to recognise the requirements of a particular martial art and the various abilities and limitations that a student possesses. There has to be a great deal of care and honesty applied in the setting of realistic targets. If they are too high, the student is constantly frustrated; if they are too low he becomes bored. You have to assess both the student and the art to judge how they are going to interrelate in the most mutually advantageous way.

The overall programme

You have to devise a programme that has an ideal long-term aim but can be broken down into intermediate targets. These targets themselves can be broken down into a series of elements. In practice the overall programme might work out as follows.

Long-term aims

The aims are:

- appreciation of the philosophy of the particular martial art
- development of the student socially and intellectually
- acquisition and development of technical excellence and its application.

Intermediate targets

The aims are:

- acquisition of grades in a systematic and progressive manner
- exposure to the various aspects of martial-arts training, grading and competition.

Short-term targets

These are the individual lessons, competitions or training opportunities to which the students are exposed.

In the planning of lessons you have to set out the long-term targets, intermediate targets and short-term targets. Using M.A.R.T.I.A.L.A.R.T. you can monitor the progress of a student in his attainment of the ideal and modify the programme if any minor or major adjustments are necessary.

10

The lesson plan and training diary

The planning and writing up of the lessons to be taught is a very valuable practice. Writing helps to clarify thoughts. The necessary mental effort required often identifies weaknesses and difficulties in planned lessons that less definite preparation would not detect. The content, form and style of such lesson notes may not entirely reflect coaching ability, but they provide evidence of the extent to which lessons have been conscientiously prepared. In the preparation of lessons, do not be too hasty to write down planned activity. Considerable reflection is necessary before deciding on a course of action. Any writing up of work is the final stage and should come only after serious consideration of students, their ability and facilities available.

In the planning stage consider the following questions.

- What is the immediate purpose of my work?
- What previous work am I assuming?
- What are we going to do next?

If you cannot give an instant answer to each of these questions, then your preparation is inadequate, and the efficiency and effectiveness of your teaching will be less than it might have been.

Planning the lesson

Plans of lessons give you information about how you propose to conduct each of them. They are not required to give details of everything you intend to tell the class or fine details of organisation. Lessons vary greatly and it is not possible to give a framework that is appropriate to all types. It should be remembered, however, that a lesson is not a haphazard series of events. It should be a structured experience, deliberately planned beforehand by the coach for a specific purpose. The art of planning a lesson is to think of it, in advance, from the learner's point of view.

Purpose of the lesson

Here you state quite precisely the purpose. This is important, because if

The coach must review each activity to ensure that it achieved its desired result. He may need to modify future practice in the light of necessary modifications

thought is given to the aim, there is a good chance that a clear impression will remain in the student's mind.

Aims should be precise and direct:

- to present competition fighting techniques
- to develop the existing standard of heinan jodan kata
- to develop a particular block
- to develop a particular lock.
- to develop a particular throw
- to develop a particular punch
- to develop a particular kick.

Lesson structure

Lessons tend to be divided into three broad areas.

Introduction

Thought should be given to how you intend to present the idea or initiate the activity.

Development

This contains the main teaching points. The part played by the students in the lesson should be carefully identified. Consider the suitability of different methods of presentation.

Conclusion

The impression left in the students' minds at the end of a lesson is very important. Lessons must not be allowed to 'peter out'; timing must be considered. Lessons may be concluded in various ways: revision exercises, final demonstration, discussion, identification of the next lesson's theme, etc.

The lesson plan

Fig. 22 shows a typical lesson plan. The format and style may need to be changed for the special needs of the coach or a particular style. However, it serves as an example of the kind of information that is important to you.

The following summary works through the plan to explain sections and the use of the information set down.

Date

It may seem obvious, but the date of a lesson is very important. Most coaches are governed by the constraints of fixed dates for gradings and competitions. It is therefore essential that a lesson is taught at the correct point in the preparation for either.

Time

Before you can plan a lesson you must consider how much time is available. Will you be able to complete all of the work that is necessary, or will there be time available for other activities? The duration of the lesson is critical when dealing with specific groups. An hour is sufficient for juniors or mature students, while an hour and a half may be necessary for the advanced and well conditioned.

Date	Time	Venue	Number in class
	Duration		Age range
Aim of lesson			Males Females
Special points to note			

	Organisation	Teaching safety points
Introductory activities		
Development		
Conclusion		
Comments		

Fig. 22 A typical lesson plan

Venue

The facility where training is to take place is very important. Any special equipment that the venue has to offer can be incorporated in the lesson. However, any lack of or inadequate facilities must be taken into account. It is no use planning practices that are not possible or potentially hazardous because of any limitations. You have to be realistic and plan only what can be safely practised.

Number in the class

The number of students in a lesson has an important effect on its style and content. There is, of course, a safety factor to be considered with large numbers. However, the number of students dictates the organisation of practice and the style of presentation. Large numbers require a much more formal setting, possibly rows, and the need for the training to consist of class drills, all the students performing the same technique at the same time. Obviously with smaller numbers there can be less formal organisation, which allows greater student–teacher contact.

Age

It is good practice to be aware of the age range in the group when devising specific practices. They may be inappropriate for juniors or more mature students. Activities or alternatives that are appropriate for all students have to be planned.

Gender

There is little difference, if any, in the development of skill between male and female students. However, you may wish to consider the suitability of certain techniques, their application and specific training practices with respect to any other relevant aspects.

Aim

Every lesson must have an aim, a purpose, to it. You may want to revise and develop existing techniques or introduce new ones. The aim of each lesson has to be carefully identified such that the work covered fits into the correct pattern of technical development and learning. Each lesson must take place in the correct sequence to ensure the most effective learning environment. Identifying the aim of a lesson ensures that this situation occurs.

Equipment

Any special items of equipment needed for any part of the lesson must be identified, booked or acquired. Forward planning in devising the work programme and the use of specialist equipment avoids any alterations to the lesson.

Special points to note

In certain activities you might want to remind yourself of particular points. They could be specific points of technique to cover that were identified in the previous lesson, or new ones. You may need to remember that new students are in the class who have not covered the techniques to be covered that lesson, or particular students with health or special problems. This section is vital as an *aide mémoire* for you, because it allows you to ensure that all students are working to the best of their ability in a positive and caring environment.

In order to produce this background information, you have to think carefully about the long-term programme for each student and how each lesson will provide the opportunity for his progressive development. In the process you will identify the activities, techniques and various practices that are required in the lesson and how they are presented. The following elements of planning are the key to effective and efficient learning and teaching.

Introductory activities

It is essential that each and every lesson gets off to a well-structured start, as it sets the tone for the rest of the session. You must take control of both students and the various activities as soon as the class enters the training area. You may want to address the class in a formal or informal way, depending upon the tradition of the school. You may want to make some important announcements or discuss the last lesson and what is to be covered in this one. It is, however, essential that you have the undivided attention of the entire class; any lack of concentration at this stage on a student's part could have disastrous consequences later on. It is good practice to establish from the start the degree of discipline that you require from students and the ground rules for training in general and behaviour and personal standards in particular.

You can plan the work that you intend to cover in this part of the lesson. The introduction usually starts with a warm-up. You should identify which exercises are to be used and which part of the body, if any, is to have special attention; this depends upon the techniques to be covered in the lesson. Although it may seem obvious, it is important that in successive lessons a range of exercises are selected during the warm-up, not only for variety but also to stop the warm-up falling into a rut.

The warm-up tends to fall into two quite distinct sections. The first part consists of general activities designed to prepare the students for strenuous physical work. Having achieved this state of readiness, you then introduce martial-art-specific exercises that are appropriate to the activities to be covered in that lesson.

Once fully prepared for martial-arts training, it is good teaching for the class to practise the main elements covered in the last and other previous lessons. In this way, not only do students continue to remember and improve the quality of their movements, they are also given a confident start to the work because they are repeating known techniques that they are familiar with. It is important that you carefully select the techniques that you are going to introduce and consider how they are to be developed in a logical fashion in this part of the lesson.

It is also good organisation to identify how the students will practise the various exercises and drills. From the class-control point of view, it is logical to start with whole-class activities, then group work that might be appropriate to their technical standards, leading on to partner work and finally individual practice. Obviously the activities have to be selected in such a way that they allow for this natural progression. This competent organisation not only adds to the effectiveness of the learning environment, it also creates a sense of order in the lesson structure. The respect for you is enhanced in the minds of the students, who see such organisation and progression in the activity as another indicator of your ability.

It is important that you make a note in your planning of particular teaching points that you want to emphasise. They may have arisen out of previous lessons' activities or be new ones specific to that lesson. Similarly, if there have been common faults or aspects of poor technique in past sessions, they should be noted. Some exercises or drills may require special consideration with respect to safety, especially with novice or mature students or ones with particular problems.

Development

Having reviewed, revised and practised known techniques, you now have a sound platform on which to build the next part of the lesson. In this section you can introduce new techniques, adapt known ones or link them into new combinations. It is important that when a new activity is being introduced, the practices that immediately precede it are well known to the student and the general movement pattern is similar to the new skill. The advantage of this strategy is that the student is confident in his own ability and has a starting point to work from. Having an existing frame of reference makes any demonstration or presentation of a new technique all the more effective for the student, because he can quickly relate it to his own existing range of skills. With similar movement patterns the rate of learning is much faster than with different ones because part of the skill is already known.

There are few, if any, differences between male and female students in the development of technical competence

You have to select techniques to be taught that are sequential to those already known by the student. As with the introduction, you have to carefully organise the practices into class, group, partner work or individual training, depending on the requirements of the skill to be taught. Once again, the lesson must 'flow', seemingly effortlessly. Any particular teaching points or aspects of class or individual safety must be identified.

Conclusion

Every lesson must have a clearly identified series of concluding activities and not be allowed to simply run out of steam. You have to identify whether you see the conclusion as an extension of the 'development' phase or a completely separate unit. For example, you may want to finish a lesson with partner work of some kind, possibly sparring, to allow the students to apply techniques learned or refined earlier. Alternatively, you may want to conclude with something completely different, such as conditioning training or games. You may wish to combine all three options. You have to identify what activities you intend to use and consider the organisation and any special safety aspects or teaching points.

Self-evaluation

The whole purpose of the planning of the lesson in this way is to ensure that you think carefully about structure and content. You will improve as a teacher only if you are able to criticise your efforts constructively. Each lesson taught should be looked at carefully, and any successes or failures should be noted and accounted for. These comments are perhaps the most important part of the planning process.

In your evaluation of your coaching you may want to indicate:

- what was actually taught, and which techniques were not covered
- what parts of the lesson were successful
- what parts of the lesson were unsuccessful
- which points could have been reinforced
- how any errors that were made could have been avoided
- if the lesson had continuity
- how better cooperation of the students could have been obtained
- if the organisation and planning were adequate
- if the lesson was appropriate to the ability of the students
- if the lesson fitted into the sequence of learning required for grading or competition
- if the various elements had a logical progression from one activity to the next
- if the planned lesson created the best possible learning opportunities

- what the students achieved.

It is vital that you consider these and other questions, particularly when preparing similar lessons for similar groups or when preparing a group for grading. Only by a process of self-evaluation can you identify which activities, styles of presentation, sequence of progressions and general lesson content are effective and, perhaps more importantly, which are not. If you identify these points over a period of time, you will develop a very effective style of teaching, retaining and refining good practice and discarding the rest. The successful planning of subsequent lessons will depend upon your ability to assess the lesson just taught.

The training diary

It is your responsibility to ensure that you plan your lessons and training programmes carefully and are aware of any students who are having particular difficulty or success. However, individual students also have a responsibility for their martial-arts development. Most sportsmen and women keep a training record of their day-to-day physical and technical programme. Such a diary contains what they did in a training session; activities that they found easy or difficult; techniques learned; special technical points to note; and any other general comments. Such a record eases your administrative load because a great deal of an individual's progress is kept on record by the student himself.

Fig. 23 shows an example of a page from a training diary. Obviously, as with the lesson plan, it can be modified for particular styles or student requirements. The sections are described below.

Date

This is obviously an important piece of information as it allows a student to identify improvement or lack of it compared to previous lessons. Also, if a student misses training his diary will show it. He then must take responsibility for his actions and not blame you for poor performance.

Time

The student might identify over a period of time that he trains better at certain times than at others. Also, he can identify whether or not he is able to give 100% for the entire lesson. This of course is invaluable information for you.

Venue

A student might find that he trains better or worse at a particular venue. Also there might be particular factors to consider such as the lighting, the

Date	Time	Venue	Coach
Introductory activities			
Conditioning exercises			
Techniques learned			
Points to remember			
General comments			

Fig. 23 A student's training diary

floor, the acoustics and/or the equipment. Any or all of these might influence training.

Coach

Some clubs use several coaches to teach a particular group. It might well emerge that a student works better or worse with a particular coach.

Introductory activities

The student can identify particular exercises that he enjoyed, found difficult or particularly beneficial or ineffective. Such information can show up specific strengths or weaknesses, be they technical or physical.

Conditioning exercises

Every student finds some of the fitness work difficult. By identifying those exercises that he finds difficult or beneficial, a student can bring to light strengths and, particularly important, weaknesses that require attention.

Techniques learned

A record of new techniques learned or modification of known ones is useful. In such a way a student is aware of what he has and has not learned.

Points to remember

This is perhaps the most important part of the diary. Here the student can carefully set down the particular technical points and comments that you have made. Obviously in the next lesson, by referring to these points, they can be worked on, making training more effective.

General comments

The student can make any observation and comments on any or all aspects of the lesson.

Lesson plans and training diaries

For some coaches the idea of preparing lessons on paper or asking students to keep a personal training record might seem 'pie in the sky'. However, there is no coach who is a parent who would expect his child to be taught unstructured lessons. Furthermore, on asking about the progress of a child in class, comments from the teacher such as, 'I'm not sure what work we have covered', 'I don't know when the exams are', or 'I don't know how your child is doing in class' would not be tolerated by any parent. Why should the martial arts be any different?

A training diary can be a most useful tool for you because you can see how effective your lessons and training plan are for each and every student. I would suggest that on a rota basis you should look at the diary, possibly with the student, and identify any problem areas.

With practice, lesson plans and training records can be completed in a few minutes, but their important can far outweigh the effort. Most martial arts emphasise self- discipline, concentration and meditation, and encourage students to study their style for the physical, spiritual, mental and technical benefits. The keeping of records of any kind is only part of that philosophy. Further, if you wish to be regarded as a professional then you have to adopt the responsibilities of the position. You may be a technical expert; you must now adopt new organisational and administrative skills to make your efforts more effective and efficient.

11

The learning process

It may seem simplistic, but the old adage, 'You can take a horse to water, but you can't make him drink', can also be applied to the willingness of a student to learn. Motivation or the student's desire to learn is the basic requirement of any progressive technical programme. The wish to learn and develop technical competence must be an inherent characteristic of any student desiring to succeed in the martial arts. The biggest problem for both the teacher and the student is that the learning process and any corresponding improvement in performance are often imperceptible!

A working definition of skilful performance might be: 'The discrepancy between the intended and actual pattern of movement'. It can be seen therefore that there is a great deal of potential for any 'discrepancy', ranging from none, as in a perfect performance, to total, in an utter, abysmal failure! Most students can very quickly reproduce a technique. It may be crude, but you can identify which skill is being performed. With continued practice of the movement and with observations and comments from you, the quality of performance should gradually improve.

Skill development

The development of any skill is an outward physical manifestation of a great many internal, interrelated physiological processes in the student's neuro-muscular systems. However, this hidden process of learning can be outwardly misleading. The fact that in one or two observed performances a student is able to perform a technique with a high degree of accuracy might be due to chance; they were 'flukes'! Similarly, one or two observed performances might show a lack of technical mastery but the other non-witnessed actions might be sound! Therefore the fact that on the odd occasion when you observe a student in the process of learning a skill, there is or is not 'observable improvement', may not fully reflect the internal adaptions or the true picture.

There is a further dimension to the learning process that has to be considered. The personal, social and environmental influences that a student is exposed to could affect the overall standard of performance in either a positive or negative fashion.

The learning of any skilled movement is not constant. Most coaches will have noticed that there seems to be an initial period of rapid learning that very soon seems to taper off. It is when the levelling-off process occurs that many students begin to lose interest and motivation in continuing to practise a technique.

Technical improvement

In the development of skilful movement and its refinement into technical excellence, there seems to be a series of progressive developmental stages, Fig. 24.

Stage one – ***have a go!***
Very much trial and error

Stage two – crude reproduction
A basic but identifiable movement emerges

Stage three – refinement of technique
Errors are corrected and the movement refined

Stage four – establishment of standard of performance
The movement pattern becomes 'grooved in'

Stage five – physical adaption
Continued practice brings about specific adaption of the body systems involved

Fig. 24 Stages of technical development: there are identifiable progressive stages in technical development

■ Stage one: a student is shown a technique and has all the essential aspects of the pattern of movement identified; he should have an understanding of the action required. He should then be able to 'have a go' at the movement. It will be very much a trial-and-error process, with good luck playing an important part in the better efforts.
■ Stage two: with practice the student becomes able to reproduce a crude but identifiable attempt at the technique required. The quality of movement may be poor, but the student can reproduce the technique at that level of excellence each time.
■ Stage three: by the repetition of the movement pattern under your critical supervision, the student is able to correct errors and refine the technique.
■ Stage four: with repeated practice of the technique, the neuromuscular systems involved physically adapt to the movement pattern.

The action becomes stable and 'automatic'.

■ Stage five: with continued practice over a period of time, not only do the neuro-muscular systems adapt, so do those elements of fitness, the 'S' factors involved. Speed, suppleness, strength, stamina and of course skill improve to produce not only a technically sound technique but one that is also effective.

How long it takes a student to progress through each phase depends upon:

- the complexity of the technique
- the existing level of skill
- the transfer of any previously learned technique to the new one
- the ease with which skills are learned
- the motivation to learn the technique
- the competence of the instructor
- the learning environment
- the student's state of physical fitness.

The learning curve

It is generally regarded that the learning of a skill follows a recognised pattern, which is usually referred to as the 'learning curve', Fig. 25. It is characterised by a rapid improvement in performance that levels off or 'reaches a plateau' after a period of time. Thereafter, improvements in the learning curve occur in a step-like manner, with relatively long periods of practice of the skill between any improvement.

The overall shape of the graph is of interest to the coach because it identifies the stages of learning. The initial rapid rise in the quality of movement is due to the student's first basic attempts becoming crude representations of the technique. Depending upon the complexity of the skill, after a few lessons the student is able to reproduce a movement that is 50–60% accurate. However, as the process of technical refinement continues, the rate of learning rapidly slows down and begins to level off somewhere around the 70–80% level.

With continued practice, there are small step-like improvements in performance that are indicative not only of the neuro-muscular grooving-in phase of skill learning, but also of the development of the 'S' factors through specific, efficient and effective training. The 70–80% level of technical excellence can be achieved relatively quickly; however, to attain the remaining 30% or 20% requires a disproportionate amount of time and effort. The 'law of diminishing returns' is applicable to the learning of skills. After a given point on the learning curve, the amount of

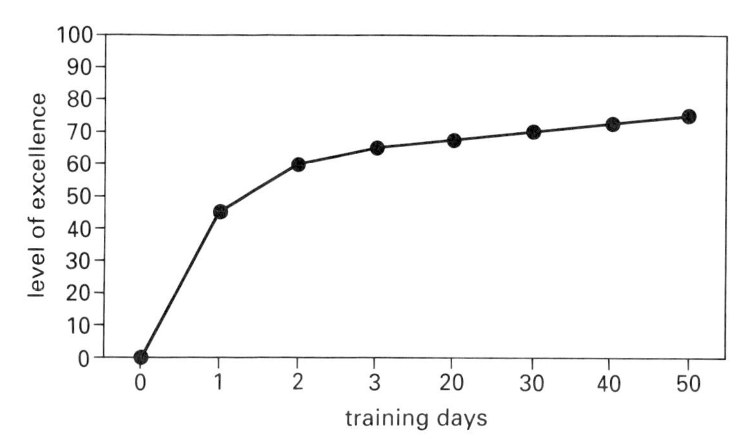

Fig. 25 The learning curve: technical improvement develops rapidly and then begins gradually to slow down

time required to bring about even a moderate improvement becomes greater and greater and disproportionate to the increase in skill levels.

In a typical situation you might initially devote 10 minutes in a lesson to teaching a new skill. After five or six lessons the students attain the 50–60% skill level. You now face a dilemma. Do you continue to devote 10 minutes a lesson, which may after 10 more lessons bring about only a 5% improvement? Or, to allow learning to continue at the same rate to achieve excellence, do you devote progressively more and more time in the lesson? Eventually this situation could lead to the entire lesson being devoted to the learning of one skill.

The alternative strategy is to teach a skill to the 50–60% level and thereafter continue to practise the skill to bring about the neuromuscular and fitness adaptions, but to accept a much reduced rate of learning, the plateau on the learning curve. The main reason for this proposal is that you have many skills to teach and, with the best will in the world, cannot spend a disproportionate amount of time on each and every technique.

The transfer of training

When teaching a new technique to a student, it is essential not to throw him in at the deep end. For effective learning of a new movement pattern, it is essential that the student can relate the new technique being learned to ones previously successfully acquired. In this way a student has an idea of what is required and has a known starting point to work from to practise and refine the new skill. A repertoire of existing movement patterns allows for a springboard from which to take off to perform the new one.

You should be aware that there is a transfer of learning from one skill to another. Similar techniques have similar requirements. Obviously when introducing a new technique, reference must be made to similar ones already learned. The correct selection and progression of techniques to be learned allow for the positive transfer of skills and for you to exploit the use of established movement patterns in the teaching and learning environment.

The 'transfer of training' means that the practice of one skill has a beneficial effect on the learning of a similar one. It is impossible for a student to practise all of the techniques already learned in every lesson. However, if you group techniques that have similar qualities, the problem can be eased. For example, all kicks that require the foot and the leg to be raised straight out in front of the student have certain common aspects of technique. The practice of any one or two has a 'carry-over' and beneficial effect, if only in a minor way, on the others. By carefully organising practice so that in a given number of lessons all of the techniques are practised in turn, it should be possible to at least maintain the existing level of performance. This procedure can be adopted for other groups and common sub-groups of kicks, punches, locks, blocks, throws, take-down techniques or weapons work.

There is a further practical reason for you to look carefully at this problem. During the rapid improvement period in skill learning, students are motivated by their rate of improvement. Their desire to learn is created by the success that they achieve. Concentration and commitment are facilitated by the rapid rate of technical development. However, once the rate of learning begins to slow down, it requires much more effort on the part of both the student and coach to maintain the attention and work rate. Eventually the levelling off of improvement begins to have a negative effect on the learning environment, which can bring about a reduction in performance.

Repetition and practice

The learning environment for the student of martial arts is practice, practice and more practice. In truth, repetition, repetition and more repetition would be a more accurate description. By repeating an action over and over again the pattern of movement eventually becomes 'grooved in'. It is therefore essential that the correct technique is both taught and learned from the outset, as if an incorrect action becomes ingrained each time the activity is practised, it will be faulty. The implication for both student and coach should therefore be obvious: only the highest quality of instruction is appropriate in the learning situation.

There are probably as many theories describing the process of learning as there are 'experts' in the area of study. In the understanding of the problem I have evolved my own 'field theory', which is based on the essential elements of the other major theories.

The field theory

Imagine a meadow in which lush grass grows. At either end of the meadow there is a stile. If you walk from one stile across the field to the other one and then turn around, you will see that where your feet trod on the grass, your route is visible. The grass is squashed and damaged by your footsteps. If you walk the same way the following week and you come to the first stile to the field, you will notice that the grass has recovered and there is no sign of you ever having been there before.

However, if you walk across the same field twice a week, the grass will not have sufficient time to recover between journeys, and by the time of your second crossing there will still be a trace, albeit a small one, of damaged grass to identify your previous route.

But, suppose you walk that same path three or more times a week, what will happen? Not only will the grass become damaged, but eventually it will also wear away into the soil and there will be a permanent record of your route across the field. Because the grass is worn totally away, even if there is a period when you no longer travel that way, your path will still be visible. There will always be a permanent mark of your presence.

So too with learning skills. If you practise a skill once a week, the various neuro-muscular pathways that are involved in coordinating the overall pattern of movement are interconnected for the period of training only. Because they are not required to constantly be in communication, they are gradually disconnected such that a week later there is no trace of their interconnections. However, should you practise the same skill twice a week, the various interconnections will not have fully disassembled by the time of the next practice, so that they can communicate more easily.

But if you practise a skill three or more times a week the various complex interconnections become 'permanent', and any time that skill is practised, it is performed both with speed and in a coordinated fashion because all of the various connections are firmly in place, ingrained or grooved in (see Fig. 26). It is in this way that skills become permanent. For a skill to be fully learned and not just a chance occurrence, there has to be brought about a physiological change in the cerebral-cortex and

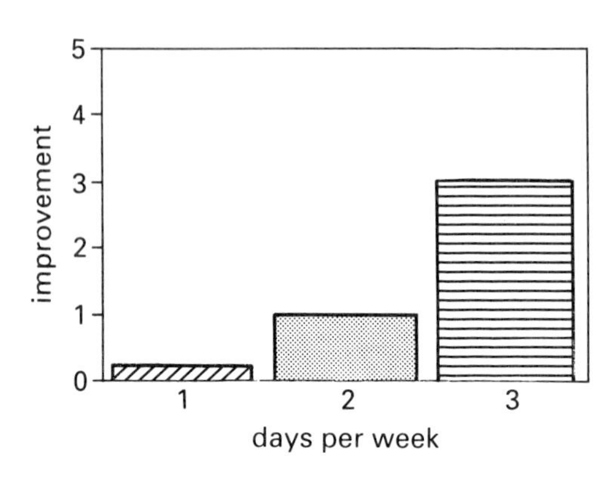

Fig. 26 The frequency of training: the number of training days per week influences the rate of improvement

neuro-muscular systems. This is why – simplistically – having learned to ride a bike or swim, even many years later it is possible to do either or both, albeit with some lack of technical excellence. The movement patterns have been permanently etched into the various body systems.

The amount of practice

Linked to the learning process and the amount of practice is the notion of how often a student should practise a technique. The 'field theory' can be of use to you in identifying the amount of time to spend on the development of any skill. The rule of thumb that can be applied is as follows.

- One practice session a week maintains the existing skill level.
- Two practice sessions a week bring about a moderate improvement in performance.
- Three practice sessions a week have a measurable positive effect on performance.

This situation may be the case with those students who are approaching or have reached the plateau phase, having established the movement pattern. However, in the early stages of skill learning, when the crude movement pattern is being developed, the effect of one lesson or more a week is far greater.

The 'forgetting curve'

When you are devising a teaching programme, one of the elements that must be considered as part of the learning process is 'forgetting'. Just as there is a 'learning curve' that you have to bear in mind, equally there is a 'forgetting curve' that is as important, Fig. 27. Even sklls that have

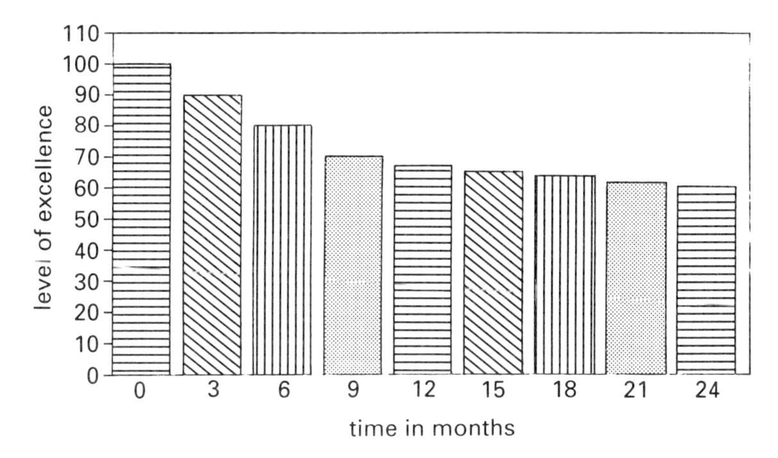

Fig. 27 The 'forgetting' curve: there is a fairly marked decrease in excellence, which gradually begins to slow down

been 'over learned' and have brought about neuro-muscular adaptions are susceptible to 'forgetting'. Basically, as you are aware, skills that approach the technical model must be practised as some form of structured training programme to maintain that level. It has been suggested that one of the reasons why some students seem to be slow learners over a period of time is in fact that they are 'fast forgetters'. This simply means that by the time of the next practice session, the various systems involved in a skill have not adapted fully, if at all, to the previous period of work.

Some recent research has suggested that two years after stopping practising a skill, assuming it has become 'grooved in', students could still achieve a 60% level of accuracy. This does seem to support the folklore that once having learned to swim or ride a bike, no matter how long the period of lay-off, 'you never forget', however shaky the efforts might be! It would appear in the forgetting process that with a sustained period away from training or practising a skill, initially there is a fall-off in the top 10% of performance. Thereafter it deteriorates at an ever slower rate until, after about two years, any further depreciation in skill levels is almost imperceptible. Though skill levels may level off at 60%, the quality of a technique or its effectiveness may deteriorate markedly. This is due to the degeneration of those 'S' factors, which are critical to the pattern of movement. It may seem simplistic, but certainly with fitness 'if you don't use it you lose it'! The specific combination of stamina, strength, speed and suppleness, which develops alongside the quality of technique, deteriorates, which gives rise to the very obvious overall fall-off in performance.

In order for the students to benefit from the 'learning curve' and not suffer from 'forgetting', you have to carefully monitor the learning environment. Too much practice can have a detrimental effect upon skill levels, as can too little. It can be seen that a long-term programme of teaching is vital in the martial arts, bearing in mind the number of skills that students have to learn.

12

Stages in the learning process

With the introduction of a new technique there is a series of phases in the learning process that you need to identify. This is an essential part of your duties if you are going to make the best use of the student's abilities and your own skills.

Level one – the elementary level

Once the student has been introduced to the technique to be taught, he is given the opportunity to attempt the movement. It is in this period that the student develops a basic understanding of the requirements of the technique and lays a foundation for further refinement.

Stage one

During the early part of the lesson, practise a technique similar to the new one to be taught that the student has already mastered. In the recovery period following the activity, discuss the new technique to be taught and its application in training, competition or the real world. Describe which techniques it resembles or has evolved from, to allow the students to relate it to previously learned movements. Because they have just practised a technique not dissimilar to the new one to be learned, they have an immediate idea of what is required. Obviously the rate at which students learn a new technique depends upon the similarity of previous actions. The closer it resembles already known movements, the faster they learn. At least in theory!

Stage two

Demonstrate the technique, identifying the essential coaching points. Give the students the opportunity to ask questions or make any comments to reinforce their understanding of the technique. It is vital that the image of the movement pattern that each student has in his mind's eye is exactly the same as that intended by you. By seeing what is required in the new activity, listening to you and identifying key points, the student is trying to create – consciously or subconsciously – a plan or sequence of his own body's movements.

Stage three

The students should be allowed to 'have a go' at the technique. The early stages of practice allow the student to try the movement plan that he constructed during the previous two stages. Quite early on in the learning process he is given the opportunity to see if it works. If the student's initial appreciation of what the technique requires with respect to his various movements is correct, then all is well. But if there are discrepancies, the plan can be reviewed and revised.

It is at this stage that your presence is essential. The student needs quite a lot of feedback in terms of the quality of his movement compared to what is required.

- Do the students think their performance resembled what was required? The loss of balance, a fall, the selection of the wrong foot or hand, or awkward movements give an immediate evaluation of their success, or lack of it.
- Through kinaesthetic feedback, students are able to be conscious of what their limbs and joints are doing during the movement, and able to compare this to their expectations and existing skills.
- Perhaps more important than the other two factors is your role in identifying the accurate and inaccurate aspects of a student's efforts when compared to the model. The feedback that you can give is not only useful, it is vital if the student is going to learn and ultimately 'groove in' the correct patterns of movement. Any inaccuracies in technique that are allowed to develop will be very difficult to correct at a later stage.

Initially in the learning of a skill there is much trial and error, but only with practice is the required technique developed. However, the repetition of a skill does not by itself necessarily bring about an improvement in the quality of movement. In fact, without your critical observation to identify inaccuracies and correct them by giving feedback, repetition on its own engrains faults, and does not eradicate them.

Level two – the transitional level

Once the student has acquired the initial crude movement pattern, he must practise to improve it. With the establishment of a positive learning environment and constructive feedback of his efforts, he can reinforce and improve good technique and eradicate errors.

Once the student has developed a basic, if crude, model of the technique, he has to understand that that is the first part of the process of achieving technical excellence. To achieve a higher standard of performance he must meet the following minimum requirements:

- the desire to want to improve his technique
- the will-power and determination to work to achieve the desired standard
- the ability to identify the correct pattern of movement required or tactics necessary in a competitive environment
- technical feedback from you as to the accuracy of his efforts
- the encouragement required for continued commitment to the training process.

The implication of the field theory for the learning environment

The learning process has to follow the neuro-muscular and cerebral adaptions that ultimately give rise to consistent excellence of performance. The stages in the learning process and the environment that facilitates them have a distinct effect upon the student's awareness of the overall movement pattern. In the early stages of learning a skill, there is much trial and error and a great conscious awareness of what all of the various parts of the body are doing at any time. It is very easy for a student at this stage to become confused or to identify and emphasise the wrong cue. Because they are in the learning process, students cannot identify if their efforts are correct or not, and are consequently reliant upon you for comment and advice. However, with repeated practice they become more familiar with the requirements and sensation of what is necessary to produce good technique. Eventually the various neuro-muscular pathways connecting muscles to their coordinating centre in the brain become more, and ultimately fully, permanent. The conscious effort needed to control the various elements involved such as limbs, muscles, joints, force and balance becomes less and less.

Ultimately the action requires no conscious effort from the student to be performed; it becomes automatic. Just as with the worn path through the field, when the skill becomes automatic, the movement patterns learned through repeated practice are brought into play without the student thinking about them. Furthermore, a student has little, if any, control of a technique once ingrained because ultimately it operates out of his conscious control. Sound instruction and input from you in the learning period is therefore essential, otherwise faults become an intrinsic part of performance.

The effects of training

With an effective teaching programme there is an overall improvement in performance that can be broken down into several clearly identifiable areas.

■ The discrepancy between the intended and actual performance gradually becomes less and less. The student's efforts resemble more closely the technical model. Technical competence and standards improve.
■ As the training process continues, the number of successful attempts in a period of practice increases. Good performance no longer occurs by chance or with luck, but because of the refinement process.
■ As movement becomes more controlled and coordinated, muscles, limbs and joints are used in a more precise fashion. Because energy is no longer wasted by unnecessary movement or effort, students find the repetition of the techniques becomes much less physically demanding. As the quality of the movement increases, the energy requirement becomes less.
■ With growing technical competence there is an increase in the co-ordination of the various parts of the body that function sequentially to produce the overall movement. With the improved efficiency of movement and the progressive build-up in forces as the various parts of the body contribute to the total action, levels of speed are increased. It is important to realise that speed of movement is a refinement of technique. Movements at speed are possible only when there is a high degree of technical excellence. Limbs and joints working in an uncoordinated fashion and generating force in the wrong range of movement are very likely to suffer injury.
■ As identified in the previous section, with an increase in the coordination of the various parts of the body that contribute to an action, the overall effect on technique is that it is performed faster. There is another dimension to the increase in the rate of movement, and that is to do with the learning process and the 'field theory'. As a pattern of movement becomes ingrained with repeated practice, so it moves from the conscious level of coordinating the movement of all of the contributory body parts in the correct sequence, which takes a measurable amount of time, to the subconscious level where all the events occur automatically. As there is no selection time wasted on controlling individual movements of limbs and joints – because all function in the correct sequence automatically – the time required to perform the action becomes measurably less.
■ As the student begins to develop technical competence, he can begin to pay less attention to his own movements. He can expect to be able to reproduce the technique with reasonable accuracy and consistency. That is not to say that he is not continuing to refine the technique, but what it does mean is that he has more time to look around and be aware of his surroundings. For example, if he is learning a block, once he has begun to master the action he can work with a partner to apply that technique.

In the very early stages, with 100% concentration on what he is doing, there would be no opportunity for him to think about the incoming blow as well. The consequence of such a situation could be quite traumatic!

■ With developments in technical competence and the application of the technique in training, grading or competition, the self-confidence of the student improves. He sees his improvements as successful efforts on his part. Success breeds success, and success breeds self-confidence. The two go very much hand-in-hand. A successful and confident student looks forward to training and enjoys the learning environment. A happy student learns faster than an unhappy one because he enjoys what he is doing and, because the skills learned are consciously and subconsciously associated with pleasure, they are retained for longer. As the reverse is also true – in that failure breeds lack of confidence and dissatisfaction with training – the learning environment has to allow for a student to succeed in what he is doing, no matter what his level of ability or competence.

■ In the latter stages of the development of technical excellence, the student can begin to utilise more of the 'S' factors in the overall action. Where strength, speed, suppleness and stamina are relevant to the skill, they can now be emphasised to enhance performance and effect. Further, each 'S' factor in its own right, where applicable, can be developed to increase the quality or effectiveness of movement even more.

Level three – the stabilised level

When the student has attained or is near to the degree of technical excellence required, it is essential that he maintains the learning programme. Skill levels need to be maintained not just for the short term, but in the long term as well. Your role is just as important at this final stage in the learning process as at any other time. The student has to be motivated to want to achieve that infinitesimally small improvement that separates good from excellent technique. This desire to continue improving the quality of movement is maintained only by the sustained, positive feedback that the student obtains from the total learning environment. No matter how competent a student becomes, he still needs to succeed, to maintain his self-confidence and motivation, and continue to enjoy training. You have a vital role to play in this situation by giving positive feedback to the student and devising productive and effective lessons.

Once a high and consistent quality of movement has been achieved, that is not the end of the process. The quality of the technique has to be maintained, not just for the immediate future – as with a forthcoming grading or competition – but for the subsequent years of training as well.

With the establishment of a skill, the student's self-confidence in both his ability in general and the performance of the given action in particular increases. He has an in-depth understanding and sensitivity for the various elements that make up the total movement. In fact he is so aware of the 'feeling' of the correct action, he can evaluate the discrepancy between his performance and the ideal. In training, grading or competition the student no longer has to agonise over the component parts; he needs little conscious effort, if any, to execute the skill with consistent proficiency. You must be alert to any complacency that might set in with a student who has achieved near-excellence. With no great challenge left, at least with a particular technique, he can soon lose interest, which is the first step on the slippery road to a lower standard.

13

Introducing a new technique

No matter how much you think you know as both a technical expert and coach, the best coaches are also perceptive and sensitive to the needs of the students. Being perceptive allows you to consider the needs of individuals, new ideas and particular situations and events with an open mind. Being sensitive allows you to assess the needs of the individual student and apply all of your technical knowledge and communication skills to ensure that he achieves the level of performance appropriate to his level of ability and aspirations.

It has been identified that the essential prerequisite for effective teaching is the acceptance of the coach by the class. Students take naturally to one who gives them a feeling of security and confidence, but one who at the same time can lead them into a new experience, be it physical or intellectual. You should show enthusiasm, friendliness, a sense of humour and a willingness to take on board the responsibility for the technical, personal and social development of every student.

Some coaching hints

- Be punctual.
- Be smart and tidy.
- Adopt an attitude of self-confidence, honesty and sincerity.
- Develop a style of speech that is pleasing to the students.
- Speak clearly and give precise and succinct instructions.
- Make use of the energy of the students and do not be afraid to join in.
- Do not talk about techniques. *Show them.*
- The self-consciousness experienced by novice coaches is the result of concentrating unduly on what *they* are going to do instead of what they want the *students* to do.

Remember this sequence when coaching.

- Get the class active as quickly as possible.
- Begin with a known activity when teaching a new one.
- Use a demonstration by yourself or a pupil.

- Comment on the performance. Give lots of encouragement and praise.
- When you stop students, *always* refer back to what they have just done; have the class repeat and do it better generally or with special emphasis on a particular point.
- Be observant and give feedback to the class and individual students.
- Add to the practice if possible.

Establish an acceptable routine for yourself and your students.

It may seem a naïve observation, but there are as many styles of coaching as there are coaches. Some are obviously more effective than others generally or in specific areas. So too with the introduction and teaching of a new technique to students. Some coaches introduce skills with little description or discussion of the new activity. This of course leads to a shambles in the following practice, because no one understands what he is supposed to be doing. Others ramble on at length, identifying the most infinitesimal detail of technique. This usually results in the students becoming bored and confused, as they are not really sure which are the main points to consider and work on. In this situation the following practice is also a shambles because of the confusion and lack of interest; however, it does not last for long because the coach has wasted most of the lesson time in his introduction!

The scenarios described obviously result in an ineffective learning and teaching environment. There are, however, several strategies that you can employ to make the best both of your students' abilities and your talents.

When introducing a new technique to students it may seem simplistic, but you have to attract and hold their attention. Some students have a very short concentration span or are easily distracted, especially juniors. In this situation your attitude is vital, as you can carry the class with you by your personality and enthusiasm for martial arts in general and the technique to be learned in particular. The self-discipline of all of the martial arts ensures that all students show courtesy at all times to their coach; however, it does not follow that they are paying attention or taking in what is said or being demonstrated!

Most coaches, individually and through the tradition of their particular martial art, develop a regular style of command for stopping the lesson and attracting the attention of the class. It is essential that this situation is maintained throughout lessons, both as good practice and self-discipline, because everyone clearly understands what is required. But, perhaps more importantly from a safety point of view, if a potentially dangerous situation arises in a lesson, on your command the activity should immediately stop, thus preventing any serious consequences.

By identifying the key elements of good practice in the teaching of a skill, a more economic, efficient and effective use of your ability and time can be achieved than otherwise.

The demonstration

Once you have the attention of the group, then what? If you wish to show them a new technique, or identify the essential aspects of a known one, how should you go about it? The traditional method of teaching and learning martial-arts skills in rows has the problem of obscuring or giving a slightly different viewpoint of a demonstration or creating hearing difficulties for students at the rear (see Fig. 28). One way of overcoming the inherent disadvantage of this method is to have the front row sitting, the second row kneeling and the back row standing. Even if the rows are staggered, there is still a problem (see Fig. 29). A variation is for the demonstration to take place in a gap between rows facing each other (see Fig. 30). These lines could also be staggered (see Fig. 31). A better organisation of the class is in the form of a semi-circle around the

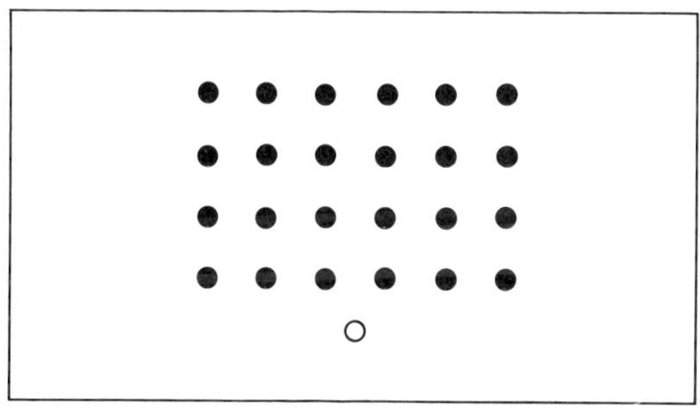

Fig. 28 Traditional class organisation: students train in regular rows

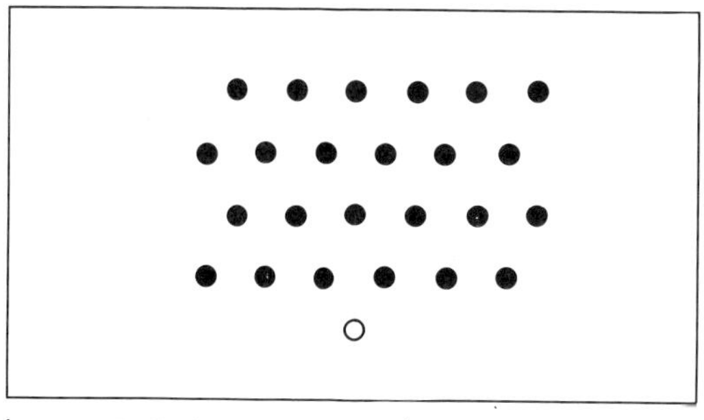

Fig. 29 Staggered rows: a variation on the traditional organisation

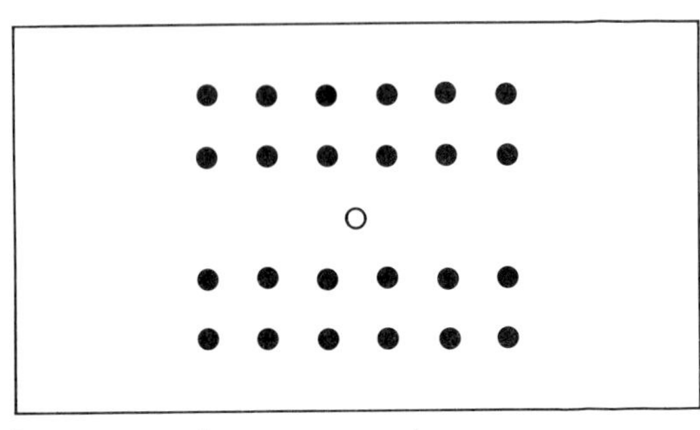

Fig. 30 Parallel rows: the demonstration takes place in the gap between inward-facing rows

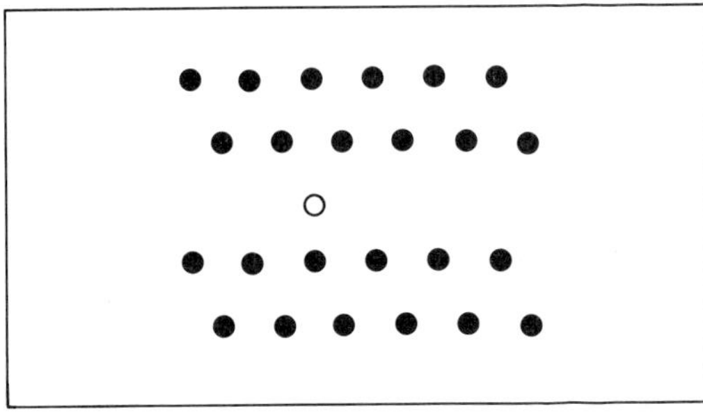

Fig. 31 Staggered parallel rows: a variation on regular parallel rows

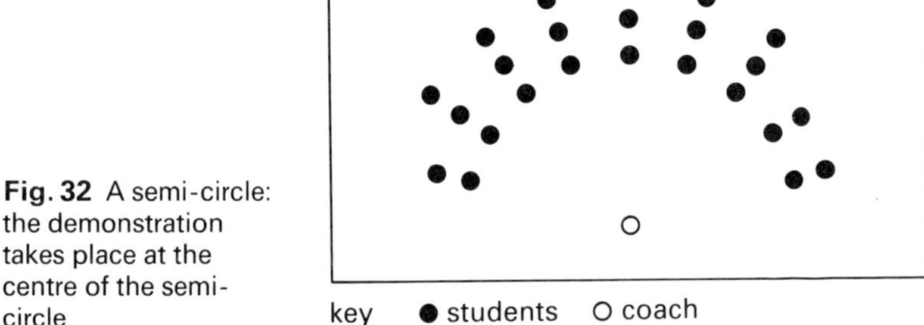

Fig. 32 A semi-circle: the demonstration takes place at the centre of the semi-circle

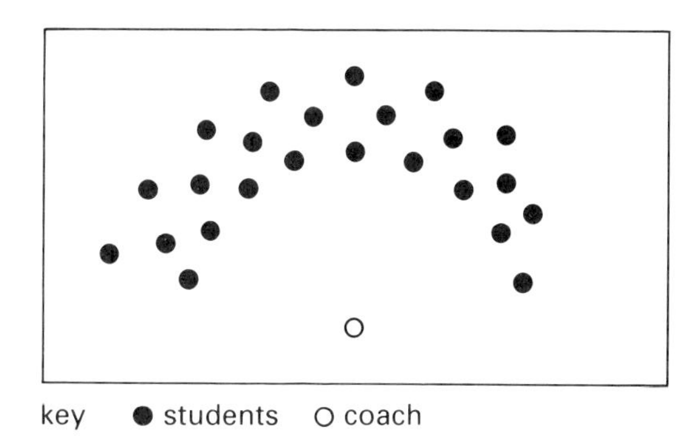

Fig. 33 A staggered semi-circle: a variation on regular rows

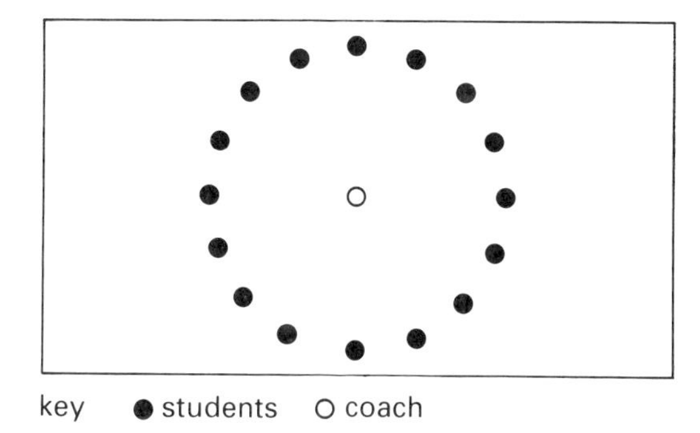

Fig. 34 A full circle: the demonstration takes place at the centre of the circle

demonstration (see Fig. 32), which once again can be staggered (see Fig. 33). Students are closer to the action and obviously have a better view of what is going on. Some styles use a full circle when demonstrating or teaching a technique; however, there are obvious limitations with this method because at any time the teacher has his back to some students (see Fig. 34).

You have to decide which class organisation – such as regular or staggered rows, semi- or full circles, sitting, kneeling or standing students, or any combination – is appropriate for the technique and the group. You must also ensure when choosing a position for a demonstration that there are no background distractions such as windows or wall charts and that it is away from any background noise such as speakers or heating systems.

With a complicated technique it may not be possible to see, hear and appreciate all that is involved from one viewpoint. There are two options open to you:

The organisation of a demonstration is vital. Coaches must be prepared to modify a technique to suit the particular limitations of students!

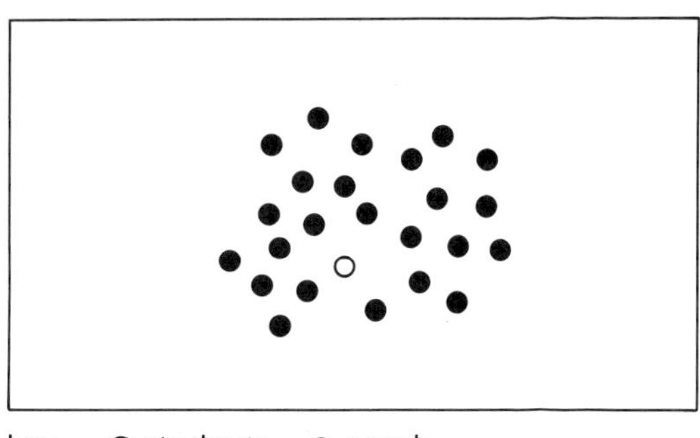

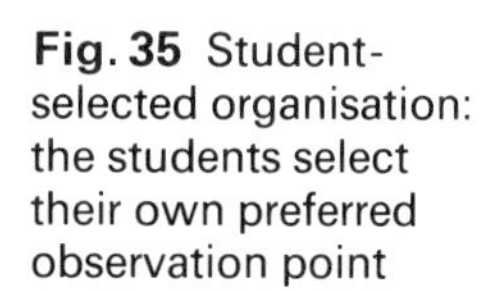

Fig. 35 Student-selected organisation: the students select their own preferred observation point

- to repeat the demonstration of the technique several times, allowing the students to move about to ensure that they appreciate all of the elements involved (see Fig. 35), or
- to repeat the demonstration with the students remaining in place but with the demonstrator changing position.

The second option has the advantage of cutting down on movement, noise and possible confusion and lack of attention to what is going on. But in some circumstances it may not be possible to change the position of the demonstrator.

However, there is a very easy way of cutting down any movement either by the demonstrator or the class. Most martial-arts facilities have access to mirrors, which are used by the students to give immediate feedback on the quality of their technique. They are an invaluable teaching aid when a student is training on his own or when you are busy with others in the group. But they can also be an innovative asset with normal demonstrations. With students in rows or a semi-circle, the demonstrator stands in front of the mirrors. Whichever view of a technique he shows the class they can, through the mirrors, see what is happening on the other side of the body (see Fig. 36).

Nevertheless, with so much visual information being presented at a time, it is essential that you focus the attention of the students on key points and don't confuse them by attempting to identify everything. It would be too simple to leave demonstrations at this point! You have to identify which are the best angles from which to demonstrate a technique to the class: the front, the side, the rear, an oblique view or a combination of them all? The more complicated a technique, the more thought has to go into its demonstration.

Equally important with the initial presentation of a new skill is who should do it. Simplistically there is no problem: the most technically

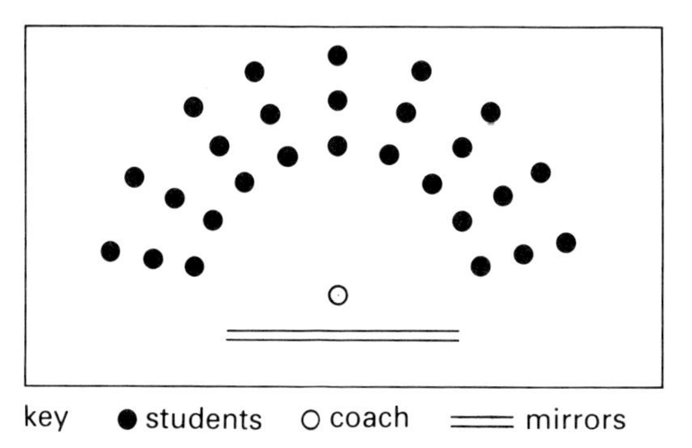

Fig. 36 Using mirrors: mirrors can facilitate an effective demonstration

competent exponent should demonstrate. Usually this would be the coach. However, it would be wrong to assume that all demonstrations require élite performers. For example, it might well be the case that a basic, but correct, execution of a skill that has no 'exaggerated elements' might be more appropriate. As such, the requirements of the action can be readily appreciated by the students as something that they can do, especially in the elementary stages of learning. It becomes a positive encouragement to learning. On the other hand, a demonstration by an élite performer that might be appropriate to an advanced exponent may be a complete 'turn-off' to a novice and create a negative learning situation. An equally important aspect to consider is that a demonstration by a student allows you to clearly identify the key aspects of performance while the movement is taking place, which is far easier and possibly more effective than you doing both at the same time.

You have to make further decisions with respect to the demonstration that are directly related to the complexity of the skill and the existing technical competence of the individual or class: should a technique be demonstrated as a complete action, or as a series of separate actions?

There really is no hard-and-fast ruling on this problem. If a simple technique is to be taught, a demonstration of the whole movement seems acceptable. Similarly, it would follow that in the students' practice of the skill they would try the complete action. With a more complex technique, it might be better to demonstrate the full technique to allow the students to understand the complete action and then break it down into separate parts. However, each section should be demonstrated and practised in sequence and learned tolerably well before moving on to the next element. Once all of the constituent parts have been learned, the technique should be performed as a flowing action. The problem with learning a skill in sections is that it can be assembled as units and performed in a jerky fashion as a series of sequential mini skills, not as a complete movement.

There are, as always, exceptions to the rule. There are some students who appreciate requirements of the most complicated techniques immediately and are able to practise the complete movement. Equally there are some students who require the most simple of techniques to be broken down into stages.

Though it seems obvious that you should pick a reasonably technically proficient demonstrator, it might not always be the case. Suppose you give a 'poor' demonstration illustrating technique being performed badly during the elementary or transitional phases of learning. You might show an error in technique of one student or a common fault within the group or make an intended or unintended mistake. This strategy might prove to be a sound platform for questions and answers, which can given an idea of the students' understanding of the pattern of movement and give them a direct feedback as to what they are doing as opposed to what they think they are doing!

With the advance of modern technology, films and videotapes have become readily available, featuring the world's best in a style or a particular technique. Obviously they do offer the opportunity for analysing skills in general or a particular technique. They have provided the student with a very useful learning medium. Students can:

- watch the film or videotape over and over again; obviously this is not possible with a live demonstration
- view techniques from a variety of angles, with more than one exponent performing the same action
- speed up and slow down, rewind and fast forward the film or tape as required to study a particular movement more carefully
- identify a specific element of technique.

However, there can be certain drawbacks to using high-tech equipment.

- Equipment is expensive and requires a great deal of technical competence to make the best use of it.
- Some venues, particularly outside ones, can be problematical. The lack of power points and the non-portability of equipment can prove to be disadvantageous.
- More often than not it is possible to see a technique from one viewpoint only.
- Showing films or videotapes takes time. Producing your own takes even longer and requires a great deal of planning and time!
- It is difficult to appreciate skill, strength, speed, suppleness, stamina and the necessary attitude, motivation and commitment involved with any physical activity from a recording.

Photographs, slides, overhead transparencies, wall charts and book illustrations can offer other teaching aids, especially for complicated or fast-moving techniques. With the novice student, they can be of use in the transitional and advanced learning situation, because they offer you the opportunity to identify the smallest detail that may be impossible to observe at normal or even reduced speed.

The conscientious coach does not identify only one visual method of explaining and showing the students the pattern of movement required. Obviously the venue, circumstances and conditions may dictate which medium of showing the technique is selected. One method by itself may be adequate, but how much more effective would be a combination of all of them!

The instructions

When introducing a new technique or speaking to the class or individuals in general, it is essential that effective instructions are given. Any comments should be brief, simple and to the point. Try to avoid long, rambling descriptions of: 'What is going to happen next' or 'What minute details to look for in the demonstration'.

Too much instruction delays the demonstration,which is the best method of showing the students what they are going to do. It bores them and distracts their attention from the demonstration, thus substantially reducing its effect. Many of the detailed comments make no sense until they have seen the technique or tried it for themselves. Such detailed

Keep any demonstration and related coaching points to a minimum. The best way to improve a technique is for students to practise under the watchful eye of the coach

technical analysis may be more appropriate in the transitional and advanced stages of learning, not the elementary one.

Any command or instruction that you give must be carefully thought out. Not only must it be clear, precise and to the point, it must also be relevant to the understanding and experience of the student or class. It is of no value if highly technical language is used with a novice or a junior; similarly, too basic a choice of words or comments are meaningless to an élite performer. As with demonstration, you must decide whether you are going to describe a complete simple technique or the separate elements of a complex one. You have to ask the question: can you describe the complexities of a technique or should you let the demonstration 'speak' for you? The adage that 'a picture is worth a thousand words' should partially answer the question. A demonstration accompanied and followed by specific but brief points to note can be very effective.

When addressing a class, once their attention has been gained it should not be necessary to shout in order to be heard. You should speak slightly louder than in a conversation, firmly and politely. You should be able to vary the sound and tone of your voice in order to project it in a clearly audible fashion. Obviously the acoustics of the training environment and the size of the group place varying demands on the amount of physical effort required to be audible. Lessons last for anything up to two hours, and you have to be heard for the entire period. This ability develops, as with all other skills, only with practice. It is very distracting to a student to have to concentrate on the squeaky remains of a strained voice towards the end of a lesson.

Presenting the technique

When considering the way in which a skill is to be introduced to a class or individual, it might be helpful to break down the presentation into its major parts for clarity, though not necessarily in the demonstration, commentary or subsequent practice.

- Briefly introduce the technique. Relate it to known and learned techniques, and identify its application.
- Demonstrate the whole technique.
- Demonstrate the preparation phase, the action phase and the completion or recovery phase.
- Demonstrate the whole action.

There should be the opportunity for the students to ask questions or make comments at any or all stages to ensure that they fully understand the requirements of the technique.

If the skill is to be practised as a complete movement, clear instructions need to be given to organise the individual or class for training. If, however, it is to be broken down into separate parts, each component must be introduced, demonstrated and then practised and learned sequentially before proceeding to the next. When all of the elements have been learned sequentially, the total movement pattern should be complete. I would suggest that as each element is learned it should form the preparation for the next one. Each element should be learned combining the preceding ones. If each part is learned in isolation, the student will have learned several mini techniques, not one complex one. As with building a wall, each brick should be laid on top of the others. If it is not, you have a pile of bricks, not a wall!

14

Feedback and assessment

As has been identified, practice or the continued repetition of a technique does not by itself guarantee an improvement in performance. In fact, unsupervised practice is more likely to introduce errors than it is to correct them or develop the quality of the skill. Your role is vital in giving the student some evaluation of the quality and effectiveness of his efforts. This process is usually referred to as 'feedback'.

Feedback is useful in several ways.

- It gives the student an immediate evaluation of the technique just practised.
- It allows for the identification of which parts of the technique were good or bad. This allows you to suggest reasons for any errors and how they might be corrected.
- The student, if given immediate feedback, can identify movement patterns with his own internal sensations (kinaesthesis), which he can quickly associate with correct or incorrect movement patterns.

The whole purpose of feedback is to help to improve the learning environment and the acquisition of technically correct patterns of movement. How you make your comments and observations known to the student can be very important. Two types of feedback have been identified: positive and negative.

Positive feedback

Comments and observations tend to be complimentary and pleasant, such as 'That was excellent technique' or 'You are working really well'. The student wants to perform the skill well, not just as part of the learning process to improve, but also to continue to receive praise from you. Often students try to please the coach, which of course has the same beneficial effect. In this environment there is no such thing as poor work. Like the curate's egg being good in parts, there has to be a saving grace in any poor performance. For example, a comment might be 'The preparatory movement was excellent but the final part was indifferent', or 'The technique was poor but the effort and the commitment were excellent'.

There is always something worthy of praise in any activity. It has been suggested that students not only enjoy praise for their efforts but also that working in an environment in which they can always achieve some success can speed up the rate of learning. They want to learn. They get a great deal of enjoyment and satisfaction out of the learning experience. It has also been suggested that students who work in an enjoyable atmosphere not only learn faster but also retain the level of skill for longer than those who work in a negative atmosphere. There is less 'forgetting'.

Negative feedback

Comments and observations tend to be uncomplimentary and unpleasant, such as 'That was terrible', 'You are making no effort at all'. They can go a stage further: 'If that is the best that you can do I suggest that you don't train again until you can ensure total commitment'. There can be an element of physical discomfort involved: 'You can stay and practise the technique until you get it right'.

The assumption is that the student associates poor work with unpleasant sensations and obviously wants to eliminate them and once again receive praise and enjoy training. Punishment is another, if not extreme, form of negative feedback. You have to be very careful in your judgement as to the value of negative feedback in the creation of an effective learning environment.

The use of feedback with junior students under the age of 16 has to be very carefully considered by you. A youngster does not respond in the same way as an adult to negative feedback. He sees the negative comments as being indicative of great personal failure, not just in the execution of the particular technique but also in the more general sense of letting down the coach, training colleagues and parents – who may have made great personal and financial sacrifices to allow him to participate in the martial arts in the first place. Out of this negative situation can develop a sense of deep guilt on the part of the student, because he feels that he is letting down everyone around him. This state of mind is created by lack of emotional maturity. Obviously this is not a healthy situation for the student to find himself in, either personally or in creating the best possible learning attitude and environment. The added emotional stress will eventually lead to very negative attitudes towards training, grading and competition, which may at best drive the student away from the activity or at worst create behavioral problems.

However, the reverse is also true. Positive feedback gives a student encouragement and a desire to be even more successful, not only for himself but also for the coach, training partners and parents. It is far better for you to give positive feedback to juniors with the immediate

The coach must try to reproduce the stresses of grading or competition in training to allow students to learn to cope with them. Performance can decline, not because students are technically incompetent or physically unprepared, but because their concentration may be affected by apparently trivial things

aim of commenting on their standard of performance. It is also good practice in the long term too, creating and emphasising a successful and enjoyable learning environment that will foster the development of a high standard of performance and very positive attitudes and standard of behaviour.

Feedback is one of the main keys to successful teaching and learning. It is a very effective method of giving the student an immediate idea of what he is actually doing as opposed to what he thinks he is doing. It is from your careful observations and measured comments that the student learns correct movements and eliminates any errors. The quality of teaching and the rate of learning are a result of the feedback given by you and the ability of the student to use such information to improve his technique or overall performance.

Realistic assessment

One of the most difficult tasks that any coach has to undertake is the accurate assessment of the ability and potential of each student. There has to be a degree of honesty between you and the student in identifying what you can realistically achieve together. Once you have identified your ultimate ambition, intermediate targets have to be set to be used as milestones on the way to that end or indicators as to how both the student and training is progressing. These targets need to be structured so that they are applicable in the short term, (the training session), medium term (the year or competitive season), or the long term (the ultimate goal)

The problem with the martial arts is that traditionally they have been concerned only with the quality of movement or success in competition. How does a coach or a student assess how they are improving week by week? Testing and measuring must be adopted by both to give indicators as to the effectiveness of the training programme and the improvement of the student. The 'S' factors of strength, speed, suppleness, stamina and skill can be assessed on a regular basis by a whole series of tests that can give an accurate measure of progress. Depending on the results, you can confirm that the existing programme is effective or modify it to achieve the desired result.

It has to be stressed that the adaption to training is slow. You and the student should not expect overnight massive increases in performance. The road to success is a long and slow one. The use of testing and measuring can identify where the student is on the road and also give feedback as to the improvement in overall performance. In the process it also helps to develop the student's confidence in both his own ability and yours.

15

Mind over matter

In the traditional style of teaching the martial arts, the acquisition and refinement of fighting techniques went hand-in-hand with the student's psychological and spiritual development. However, as all aspects of sport and leisure have become more commercialised, the financial and social rewards of success have achieved a high level of importance in the minds of the participants. The martial arts, despite their philosophical and religious associations, have not escaped such commercialism. One has only to look at the many combat-sports magazines to see the potentially lucrative opportunities for successful martial artists. These range from the promotion and endorsement of clothing, equipment, books, videotapes and films, to coaching clinics and the setting up of their own school or style of martial art. When one considers that there are over 300,000 students in regular training in the martial arts in the U.K., it is evident that there is a massive potential market for such commercial ventures.

To obtain these materialistic rewards, many instructors and their students seek any means of acquiring that extra level of performance that will give them that winning edge. However, along with the materialists the student with traditional values and attitudes towards his style has to adopt a similar approach if he is to compete. Even those students who are not involved in the competitive scene are influenced by trends in training and performance. Technical excellence and physical condition have long been seen as vital components in the overall picture of performance. However, all things being equal, with two equally matched students the one who is better prepared psychologically has that vital edge. Since the 1950s and the innovative work of Hans Selye, psychologists have studied sport and the demands and effect it has on the individual. Today the role of the 'sports psychologist' has subtly changed; it now offers sportsmen and women an opportunity to 'condition' their minds for the many stresses of training, grading and competing in sports, including the martial arts.

There are very few dedicated martial artists who would deny the importance of developing and achieving the correct state of mind for training, grading and competition. However, in the normal lesson or training session there is very little, if any, specific psychological preparation. Any improvement in a student's attitude, commitment and tolerance to stress occurs as an incidental bonus. There are those fortunate individuals to whom fate has given all of the mental and physical prerequisites for excellence, but these are the exceptions. For the 'average' student, though you might prepare him physically, his lack of success at whatever level might be directly attributable to a total lack of psychological conditioning. Think about the following questions.

- Why does a student always win in Carlisle, no matter who his opponent may be?
- Why can a student never beat a particular opponent, even though technically and physically he is superior?
- Why does a student always perform at the peak of his ability when there is a crowd?
- Why is a fluffy teddy-bear mascot an essential part of a student's kit when grading or competing?
- Why does a student, no matter how hard he tries, get a particular technique wrong?

Every coach and student could describe several similar examples.

In the training process you have to identify the psychological elements that a student needs to develop or control to allow him to achieve his potential. It cannot be stressed strongly enough that this does not apply only to élite performers. All students, no matter what their level of competence and aspirations, can improve if they work on the appropriate psychological aspects.

Modern sports psychology has identified several areas of special interest for both coach and student with respect to mental preparation for the martial arts. These are the ability of the student to:

- reduce physical stress through relaxation
- reduce mental stress through relaxation
- improve self-confidence
- improve concentration
- realistically identify and assess his ability to achieve his targets in training, grading and competition
- mentally rehearse the techniques and stresses that he will experience during actual performance
- identify the best strategy to put him in the ideal psychological state for performance.

There can be no exact order of importance for these elements as it would depend upon the specific requirements of each student. Some might need all of the elements, while others might need to develop only one or two. You must decide those areas that a student needs to develop.

Relaxation

Everyone involved in the martial arts is aware that the psychological and physical stresses of training, grading and competition can create tension in both student and coach alike. This can range from a tightening of muscles to an inability to remember and coordinate patterns of movement. Obviously any factor that affects performance, be it physical or psychological, needs to be identified and controlled. The fact of the matter is that both aspects are closely interwoven in the process of creating tension.

There are several strategies to help a student, or a coach, to overcome stress. The following relaxation techniques are aimed at trying to get the student to imagine or visualise and concentrate on less stressful images.

■ The student concentrates on the contraction and relaxation of muscle groups throughout the body. Normally he lies on the floor with his eyes closed. He then starts to alternately contract and relax muscle groups throughout the body, usually starting with the toes and slowly working up towards the neck and head. Your soft, quiet, soothing and reassuring voice identifying the muscle group to work on not only reduces muscular tension, it has a calming effect as well. Contraction and relaxation periods should last somewhere between 15 and 20 seconds, with a pause between muscle groups, taking two to three minutes to move from the feet to the head.
■ This technique concentrates on the student's pattern of breathing. Again he lays on his back on the floor with his eyes closed. Under your gentle instruction, the student concentrates on slowing down his rate of breathing and being aware of the beating of the heart. A state of calm is thereby created.
■ The student imagines that he is in a warm, cosy and safe environment. Often the student might be asked to imagine that he is in an idyllic setting, for example in a warm, sunny meadow. By visualising and concentrating on the mental images of the grass, flowers, trees, bees, warmth and contentment, the student is 'transported' into the location and away from the stresses of the immediate situation.
■ A similar strategy involves the student creating mental images of familiar scenes such as a room or office. The student is asked to concentrate on building up an accurate picture of the room, carefully concentrating on its size, shape, decorations and furnishings. Again, by focusing the student's thoughts in such a way, the stresses of the immediate situation are reduced or forgotten.
■ The 'stress box'. The student is asked to concentrate on visualising a

room with no furnishings except for a wooden box with a lid, sitting in the middle of the floor. The student then visualises entering the room, going to the box and opening it. In his imagination he writes on a piece of paper the greatest anxiety that he has at the present time, puts it into the box and closes the lid. He is now able not to worry about that problem because he can come back to it after the present stressful situation is over. The student can make several more visits to the box, each time to place another problem into it.

- The student repeats key words or phrases. These include the repetition of mantras or quotes such as 'When the going gets tough, the tough get going'. Listening to music or reading and reciting poetry or literature that is soothing and calming can also be useful.

Though any of these techniques can be used on their own, normally several of them would be amalgamated into a programme of relaxation. Obviously individual students benefit from one technique more than another and must experiment with the various systems to identify which seems to work best for them. In the normal martial-arts situation, you would create class activity based on relaxation, but with practice and experience the student should be able to work through the appropriate strategy on his own, anywhere and at any time.

A word of caution! These relaxation techniques create a state of calm and well-being and reduce tension. They also lower levels of aggression. It could be quite possible to 'overdo' the relaxation if aggression is required. You and the student must take this aspect into account when identifying the need for and extent of relaxation strategies.

Self-confidence

Self-confidence is based to a large degree on the student being successful. Everyone wants to succeed, and success spurs people on to want to achieve more. In order for the student to be successful, the targets that are set for him must be realistic and within his capabilities. It does not matter whether you are dealing with a student who competes at international level or one who just enjoys training. His continued enthusiasm in the activity will be based not only on progressive and systematic training, but also on his and your ability to identify realistic and attainable targets. These could vary from the mastery of a new technique to the winning of an Olympic gold medal. If the student can regularly achieve success in a well-structured programme, his self-confidence in his ability, at whatever level, is reinforced.

It may be obvious, but unrealistic targets put the student in a 'fail situation'. Once on this slippery slope, he quickly finds himself question-

Training can be fun! Students who enjoy their training learn faster and, being motivated, learn more than their disinterested counterparts. In this way they can quickly develop both technically and, perhaps more importantly, personally

ing his ability in everything that he does. This brings about not only a lack of self-confidence but also a real lowering of performance levels.

Confidence-building can come from two main sources: firstly, from within the student himself. Through training he develops a belief in his own ability to achieve success. Secondly, this can be reinforced by positive encouragement from you and others close to the student. Both internal and external belief in a student's ability is the key to success. However, the lack of one or the other or, worse still, both, will have disastrous consequences.

Concentration

In the martial arts, concentration usually refers to the student's ability to focus all of his attention on one specific task. However, it is far more complex than that. Is the act of concentration required the same to generate maximum force in the shortest possible time, requiring excellence of movement (as in breaking techniques) as it is for balance, control and quality of movement over a sustained period (as in katas, patterns or forms)? Is concentration the same in the demands of training, grading and competition? Concentration is not a constant mental capacity; there are different types. However, it is essential for excellence of performance at whatever level. The art of developing concentration is to learn to ignore distractions and clear the mind of all other thoughts except for the task in hand. Carefully structured training programmes can recreate the pressures of grading and competition to allow the student to improve his concentration.

There are mental-imaging strategies that the student can try. These can involve complicated mental mathematical computations for short or long periods. Alternatively they can involve continued repetition of single or multiple techniques, either in the mind's eye or in actuality.

Mental rehearsal

Traditionally in all sports, including the martial arts, the preparation for training, grading and competition was the ubiquitous physical 'warm-up'. Whereas it has long been accepted that the student thoroughly and systematically increases his body temperature and the function of the various body systems involved in demanding physical activity, it is only recently that it has been realised that the various psychological elements required need similar preparation.

Mental rehearsal involves the student visualising himself performing the single action or sequence of techniques. Once he has established this mental image, he attempts to physically 'feel' himself performing the action correctly. This strategy can be used as part of the relaxation or concentration elements prior to the activity or in the breaks between periods of action (see Fig. 37).

State of mind

What is the best state of mind for the student to allow him to succeed? Quite simply it varies from student to student and activity to activity. The 'psyching up' of students is by its nature a very individual process. What puts one individual into the correct mental state reduces another to the point of abject failure. A thorough understanding of the student is an essential prerequisite for you to assess the correct level of arousal for him; too little or too much could prove disastrous in terms of perform-

- Try to visualise both performance and outcome
- Try to be aware of even the smallest detail
- Try to physically feel the movements and stresses
- Visualise the positive aspects only
- Visualise the technique (1) in slow motion (2) at speed
- Visualise any technique for 2–3 minutes before practice
- Try to visualise techniques in rest periods during training
- During rest between training sessions or while injured, try to visualise techniques
- Use visualisation to prevent boredom
- Use visualisation after performance to identify discrepancies in technique

Fig. 37 Visualisation

ance and confidence. Most systematic preparation strategies include the best strategy for raising the student to the best mental state.

Whereas 'psyching up' can be advantageous for the student, the 'psyching out' of an opponent can be the opposite. Strategies designed to undermine the confidence and performance of an opponent can be counter-productive. In the first instance, they may not work and may in fact inspire the opponent to greater efforts. In the second instance, if a student is concentrating on what an opponent is going to do, he is not directing all of his attention to what *he* is going to do. Consequently his own performance is diminished. Any student has enough to do to apply all of his potential to the task in hand, without worrying about what anyone else is doing.

It is not that many years ago that it was noticed that some of the 'Eastern bloc' athletes not only had a fixed programme of preparation prior to performance, but that they even acted like automatons. They went through exactly the same warm-up and specific preparation each time they competed. They even took their tracksuit and outer garments off in exactly the same order each time. Furthermore, they seemed totally oblivious to any external factors, such as the crowd or the other competitors, that might affect their performance. Though this might seem an extreme form of mental preparation, no one can argue with the success of the various Eastern bloc sportsmen and women in international competition.

The employment of any of the strategies described should not turn any sportsman or woman into an automaton but rather create an ability to control his psychological state to enhance – not hinder – performance. These mental 'skills' can be developed just as the physical ones. And just like the physical ones, mental skills need to be practised on a regular basis if they are going to improve. As part of the lesson or training session, at the start or end, some of these mental skills could be included in the warm-up or cool-down. At least 10 minutes should be set aside for such mental training. Imagery could be used before and during some of the more demanding practices. Just as with the adaption of the body to physical demands of physical activity, it does take time for the body to respond in a similar fashion to these mental training strategies. The preparation phase of the training cycle offers an ideal opportunity for a student to learn these mental skills. This means that as time becomes more valuable in later phases, only a short maintenance programme needs to be followed to maintain the acquired level of control.

Conclusion: theory into practice

The previous sections have identified the theory of teaching martial-arts skills and how it can be put into practice. It is quite clear that technical or performance development is dependent on the learning environment. It is vital therefore that you are aware of that process. Apart from the desire to learn fighting skills as an end in itself, the overall aim of training is to perform techniques in the grading, competition or real-life situation. Obviously it is both prudent and good practice to isolate these movements so that they can be learned and developed in the safety of the training environment.

The learning process

To facilitate the learning process, the various elements are drawn together below in a concise form and the essential elements of good practice are identified.

Learning the techniques

In the process of learning and refining martial-arts skills, there seems to be a series of progressive developmental stages.

- Stage one: the student develops an understanding of the action and is able to produce a basic movement pattern.
- Stage two: the student is able to reproduce a crude but identifiable technique.
- Stage three: by repeating the action under your supervision, the student is able to correct errors and refine the technique.
- Stage four: with repeated practice of the technique, the neuromuscular systems involved adapt to the movement pattern. The action becomes automatic and stable.
- Stage five: when a technique is repeated on a regular basis, those 'S' Factors involved – speed, strength, stamina, suppleness and skill – also adapt, producing not only an action that is technically sound but one that is also effective.

With young martial artists there is an added dimension to the learning of effective techniques, that of maturation. Those techniques that require speed, strength, power and range of movement will only be mastered when particular physiological characteristics have naturally developed.

Skills to be learned fall broadly into two categories:

- Closed skills: these are those techniques that are performed by the student as a response to a specific stimulus. Classically these skills are practised by repetition in class lines.
- Open skills: these are those skills that are performed where there is possibly a whole series of changing factors that can affect performance.

The implication of the nature of skills can be exemplified by students learning skills in class lines but then having to apply them in the grading and competitive environment, where there are many distractions, stresses and constantly changing situations in which the techniques have to be performed accurately, efficiently and effectively.

In the learning process there is an initial rapid improvement in the quality of technique as a result of effective practice. The rate of improvement gradually slows down until a plateau is reached. Repeated practice eventually produces a further slight improvement before another plateau is reached. Progress is made in this step-like fashion.

Instruction

It is essential that technically correct movement patterns are learned and practised from the very start of training. This depends totally upon your ability to effectively communicate the essential elements of good technique to the student – visually, verbally or physically.

Practice

You may identify how often a technique should be practised, how many times in each session it should be repeated and, perhaps more importantly, and often overlooked, how much rest is required. This varies from student to student, depending upon how best they learn, their levels of fitness, the complexity of the technique and the intensity of the workload.

Whole or part-whole learning

Should a technique be taught in one complete action or broken down into a series of segments that can be learned individually, then reassembled into the whole movement? This depends upon the complexity of the technique involved, the skill level of the student, the ability to learn new skills, the level of fitness and possibly age and sex.

Age

Physiological development varies with respect to age, and there are very critical changes around the time of puberty and towards maturity. Early skill acquisition should therefore be geared towards basic movement patterns involving body coordination and interaction with the environment. Specialisation should not take place until after puberty, as motor coordination improves towards maturity. With the more mature martial artist it is the rate of learning that is the main factor, not the skill.

Gender

There are physiological changes related to the post-puberty period that identify differences between the sexes; however, the rate of skill acquisition is not markedly affected. In western culture some activities involving females may be negatively influenced.

Retention

Techniques that are 'overlearned' are retained better than those that are merely 'experienced'. You must accept that a certain amount of 'forgetting' occurs in terms of the quality of performance from lesson to lesson, but this is not a major factor. Students develop skills better in a pleasant learning environment than in an unpleasant one.

Transfer of training

The development of a specific technique can be attained only by practising that specific skill. The practice of other skills might have a positive effect on development but not to a marked degree. Specific training leads to the application of that skill in highly specific situations whereas general training provides many more options.

Skill learning

This involves the physical modification of the neuro-muscular processes assumed to take place whenever a change in performance is exhibited that is not due to growth or fatigue. There is an actual physiological change in the cerebral cortex. Ensure therefore that the correct technique is taught from the start.

The coach's personal qualities

For there to be the best possible opportunity for students to learn, you must possess, in various degrees, a great many personal qualities such as the following.

Communication skills

For effective coaching you need:

- a body of knowledge
- personal standards
- demonstration
- explanation
- sensitivity.

Organisational skills

In terms of organisation, the following elements are important:

- observation
- planning and recording
- lesson organisation
- psychology
- physiology.

The learning environment

In the learning environment you must:

- give a clear demonstration of the technique to be practised
- emphasise key points with concise explanations
- begin and end all explanations with key learning points
- relate any new skills to any known ones
- demonstrate simple techniques as one whole action
- if necessary, break complicated techniques into parts to be assembled into the whole movement
- make techniques relevant by showing their application
- remember that learning techniques causes them to become 'grooved in' and performed without conscious effort
- remember that too much time between training leads to 'forgetting'
- only practise skills when the student is fatigued if he must perform them in similar situations.

And when analysing technique, you should:

- compare the student's effort with the correct technique
- correct only one error at a time
- identify the cause of the error
- identify the correction of the error

If the coach is sensitive to the abilities and needs of each student, and he devises an effective learning environment, the technical, tactical, physical and psychological benefits which are associated with the martial arts will inevitably be achieved

- consider if the student is capable of making a correction
- ask whether the student is motivated to improve his technique
- consider changing a technique only if it is fundamentally unsound, unsafe or affecting performance
- praise effort and sound technique
- give simple and precise feedback
- motivate the student.

After a period of training, grading and possibly competing in his chosen style, each student should be able to:

- identify his own levels of aspiration
- critically assess his own success or failure
- experience interaction and communication within groups
- experience dependence on other group members
- 'manage' the spirit of competition with others, alone or as part of a group
- 'compete' with himself
- understand the philosophy of his martial art
- understand his obligation to his style with respect to personal responsibility, authority and discipline
- be aware of the potential danger of using his fighting skills outside the training, grading or competitive environment
- experience participation in the martial arts as a means of communication and self-expression.

The five commandments of coaching

In very simple terms there are five golden rules for you to follow:

- DEMONSTRATION: by you, student, film, video or any other means to reinforce key points of technique.
- COACHING POINTS: build up students' understanding of a technique with concise explanations of key points.
- QUESTIONING: ask the students if they understand and let them ask about any points that are unclear to them.
- OBSERVATION: critically assess the efforts of the students.
- ENCOURAGEMENT: enthuse the students to want to train; make the lesson interesting and enjoyable.

If you, the caring and conscientious coach, follow the guidelines identified, you will be able to fulfil the ultimate aim of coaching, which is: 'To offer each student the opportunity to follow a training programme that is appropriate to his own individual ability, aspirations and commitment'.

Index